Ethical Ambition

DEC'03

Dear Dawne,

Man won achieve
rould wish
if.

Kind thoughts,

Peter

Ethical Ambition
Living a Life of Meaning and Worth

Derrick Bell

BLOOMSBURY

For Janet Dewart Bell
and in memory of
Derrick Albert and Ada Elizabeth Bell
and
Jewel Hairston Bell

First published in Great Britain 2002
This paperback edition published 2003

Copyright © 2002 by Derrick Bell

The moral right of the author has been asserted
Bloomsbury Publishing Plc, 38 Soho Square, London W1D 3HB

A CIP catalogue record is available from the British Library

ISBN 0 7475 6454 X
10 9 8 7 6 5 4 3 2 1

Typeset by Hewer Text Ltd, Edinburgh
Printed in Great Britain by Clays Ltd, St Ives plc

CONTENTS

Throughout the ages, men and women of senior years, ignoring the outward greed and inner narcissism that held their worlds enthralled, have counseled ethical living as the proper road to a fulfilling life. Strange? Paradoxical? Bizarre? Yes, all of these, and yet here I add my voice to concur in what I've learned is basic truth.

D.B.

INTRODUCTION

How can I maintain my integrity
while seeking success?

THOSE OF US with ambitions and dreams of success struggle with this question every day. I have never ceased grappling with it, and I know its implications are a source of ongoing concern for many of my students, whether they are students of color, white students with progressive politics, or students who see themselves as marginalized in other ways. They are worried about the choices they've already made, or the ones they are afraid they will have to make as they gear up to pursue individual success in a competitive marketplace. Many of them have already witnessed unfairness and perhaps have even been its victims. They realize the price of a life lived with integrity may be high, particularly if they have corporate aspirations. How are they to achieve their goals without compromising their identities − without sacrificing their sense of who they are?

Often they see *my* life as an answer to these questions. They and others who seek my advice assume that I have the

1

solution to their career dilemma because my status as a law professor was not derailed when, in order to protest the lack of minority women as faculty members, I gave up a tenured position at the Harvard Law School, and earlier, for similar reasons, a deanship at the University of Oregon Law School, Surely, having survived after walking away from prestigious jobs, I must have the answer to how they can achieve success with integrity. Without intending it, I have become a model for many, even a hero to some. This elevated status carries with it an obligation to share honestly the meaning of my experiences. This obligation extends beyond just my students, other lawyers, and activists. I direct my words to them, but just as much to anyone who is striving to do well *and* do good, and especially to those who can't imagine it might be possible to do both.

I want this book to encourage those who, by reading it, may recognize more clearly their abilities, talents, and potential for positive contributions in this world. A committed life need not mean one without fun, without laughter, without romance. Energized with this insight, readers may better see that a full life should include humor and good times while challenging the barriers that life poses. This all-encompassing approach can nourish the spirit — whatever the risks, whatever the outcome.

Students know I was not to the manor born. I come from a working-class family. Neither of my parents got beyond high school. Only one member of my extended family — an uncle living in a different city – completed college and earned professional status. I did not graduate from a major college or law school. I didn't go on from there to a prestigious judicial clerkship. I really resigned from my first job in the Civil Rights Division of the U.S. Justice Department because they viewed my two-dollar NAACP membership as a conflict of interest, and insisted I give it up. Then, after a stint serving as director of my hometown chapter of the NAACP, I joined the NAACP Legal Defense Fund and worked in the Deep South as a civil rights lawyer. In subsequent positions, I administered civil rights and poverty law programs. These are hardly credentials likely to excite the pulses of hiring personnel at an elite law school. However, in the wake of the urban disturbances that followed the assassination of Dr Martin Luther King, Jr, and the student protests of the time I was invited to teach at the Harvard Law School, and became the first black person to gain tenure there. I've written a half-dozen books that look hard at racism – far from the ideal subject matter to enhance a reputation at a premier law school.

After a decade at Harvard, I left to accept the deanship at the University of Oregon Law School. Five years later, I resigned after the faculty voted that I could not offer the position to an Asian American woman who had been placed third on a long list of candidates after the top two choices turned it down. At the time, most of the school's minority students were Asian Americans, and we had no Asian

American faculty members. I returned to Harvard for five years. Then, in an action that received a great deal of public attention, I took a leave without pay to express my disappointment with the school's failure to appoint a woman of color to the faculty. When after two years, I refused to return, citing the school's failure to act on my protest, Harvard dismissed me and forfeited my tenured position. And yet, I am still teaching and writing, now at the New York University School of Law. Leaving jobs and engaging in other activities to protest what I felt was wrong did not destroy my career. To the contrary, those actions, while not always easy to take, enriched my life and provided me with the perhaps unrealistic but no less satisfying sense that I was doing God's work.

Obviously, mine is a most unusual professional journey. As one student put it, "You're a scholar, but you're also an activist. How many other activist-academics are there, black or white? Not many. You are viewed in some quarters as a racial troublemaker, but you have the respect of people across racial lines." Like many who discuss their future with me, the student wanted to know how I did it. Responding to the question with "I was very fortunate," while certainly true, would not do. Those who ask feel I have defied too many class and race barriers that appear to them insurmountable. They want answers, not expressions of humility.

It's harder to describe an approach to life than simply

review a résumé. Given the successful ends, it is tempting to assert that I set a clear course with well-defined motives right from the start. Tempting but far from the truth. Many of the decisions that led to what my students see as worthwhile outcomes were not easy to make and seemed as likely to lead to the abyss as to advancement. Going in a direction other than — often in opposition to — the mainstream is often unnerving. I did benefit from the support of a strong family, a wonderful wife, and helpful teachers and role models. No less important was a developing belief that life offers a spiritual foundation of support for difficult decisions, and the actions based on those decisions.

Far from seeking designation as a saint, I am ambitious and I am not averse to pursuing success. I certainly have faults and have not, moreover, sought to be different just for difference's sake. I much prefer harmonious relationships to confrontational ones. I have worked for success as the world measures success, but my primary goal has been to live an ethical life, or as the hymn puts it, "to live the life I sing about in my song." That means I try to choose the ethical route even when defeat rather than success may wait at the end of the road. In fact, just as I know victory based solely on might is no victory, it is also hard for me to imagine truly fulfilling success that isn't the result of ethically founded, sustained endeavor.

The students and others I meet are certainly not looking to me for advice on how to become wealthy or powerful.

Rather, while they hope for financial independence sufficient to enable them to live comfortably and provide for their families, they really want to know how they can make a contribution through work on any number of social, political, and economic issues that burden many while advantaging a few. In short, they want their professional and personal lives to make a positive difference to others and therefore to themselves.

For those who approach me, these are not abstract inquiries. Many of my students are facing the repayment of college and law school loans totaling upward of $150,000. Yet heavy debt loads and family obligations have not pushed them into accepting high-paying jobs in large corporate law firms. They willingly accept less than a third as much in often hard-to-find positions with a public interest law firm, a district attorney's or a public defender's office. I admire their idealism while wondering whether had I the opportunities available to them, I would have chosen civil rights over corporate practice. My admiration aside, these students fear that idealism alone in a get-ahead-at-any-cost world will not provide sufficient insulation for even their genuine commitment.

They have reason to be concerned. I have been an activist for social justice throughout my professional career. I learned the hard way that material success is more important for most people than justice, at least when the former is perceived to be in conflict with the latter. It is all too easy to have the most worthy aims distorted by economic and social pressures into measures of success that can be deposited in the bank. Getting to be number one is not a goal limited to the athletic field. In this so-called free enterprise society, competition is the name, and moving on up – often by any means necessary – is the game.

In an economy that swings from boom to bust with alarming regularity, just staying even is a challenge. Corporate mergers, consolidations, restructurings, downsizings, to say nothing of nefarious business practices – all are capable of wrecking career plans of those in executive or middle management positions, as well as destroying the means of lower-wage earners and the peripherally employed to support themselves. When income sources are taken away or endangered, ethical standards as well as financial stability are placed at risk. Unlike major corporations, we can't turn for relief to provisions in the tax code or influence with legislators to bail us out. We find ourselves falling off the ladder of rising expectations without golden parachutes to cushion our landing.

We wish fervently to believe that America was founded on and has lived by ideals of social justice. In that effort, we expend great amounts of psychological energy trying to ignore a national history of eager exploitation of those on the bottom – no matter who they are. Our dominant media, themselves dominated by corporate sponsors, downplay economic disparities while constantly urging us to believe that we are good and that we are even better when we view monetary success as an end in and of itself. It is hardly surprising that so many promise and so few follow through on their pledge that "once I have made mine, I will be able to do some good in the world." Nor is it a surprise that even those who are flat out going for the brass ring of success, as traditionally defined, can be simultaneously lured by and leery of it. This is so even as the craving to "make it" becomes a compulsive obsession, and an unquestioned but no less fearsome motivating force in our lives.

Let's face it. We live in a system that espouses merit, equality, and a level playing field, but exalts those with wealth, power, and celebrity, however gained. Tremendous disparities in income and opportunity are generally accepted. Those disadvantaged by the system who *should* challenge the status quo are culturally programmed to believe that those who work hard, make it; and for those who don't make it, well that's just the breaks. Our nation's leaders, with few exceptions, are committed to getting ahead regardless of the cost to others. They may espouse ideals of social justice and equality on celebratory occasions, but then support or refuse to challenge policies that enhance the power of the already powerful.

It is hardly surprising that Americans as a people experience so much ambivalence about what we want out of life. The tragic events of September 11, 2001, have forcibly injected serious doubt into this already confused muddle.

The sudden deaths of so many have stopped us in our ambitious tracks. Beyond grief, fear, and despair, what is the message that we should take to heart? While we strive to unscramble life's imponderables, the major interests and their political representatives scheme to turn tragedy into profit – political and economic. Caught up and seemingly helpless in such moral malevolence on all sides, we search for sources of strength that will save us from terminal despair. If, in addition to terrorist attacks, we must contend with an America that is racist, sexist, and homophobic, with ever-widening gaps in income, wealth, and opportunity, how is it possible to achieve a balance between ethics and one's profession or work when the accepted wisdom is that one or the other must be sacrificed?

I have not found a life map or simple five-step plan with which to guide myself safely through the many disappointments and delusions of modern life. The temptations are many, and come in all manner of seemingly innocent forms. Recognizing them for what they are and then rejecting them is a continuing challenge. Experience has taught me that the recognition-and-rejection process, never easy, can be made feasible by modifying ambition's drive with a carefully nurtured ethical component. Through *ethical ambition*, I have found it possible to avoid compromising myself at every turn to get ahead. Trying to simultaneously balance my dreams and needs is tough, and requires an ongoing assessment of who I am, what I believe, value, and desire.

This is easier to say than to do, because what I value and what society tells me I should desire often clash. And it is frustrating to recognize that adherence to my beliefs and convictions seems to stand in the way of my material goals. Believe me, I have every reason to understand why so many simply "go with the flow," stifling pangs of conscience with hopes of personal gain.

The challenge is to consider and then put aside the consensus view of how to get ahead. I have found it scary and exhilarating to commit my energies in support of my beliefs, manifesting those beliefs by practices that enable me to honor my values while keeping faith that my needs will be taken care of. Whatever your faith − or lack of it − I find something reassuring in the biblical response to human anxiety: "Consider the lilies of the field, how they grow; they toil not, neither do they spin. And yet Solomon in all his glory was not arrayed like one of these" (Matthew 6:28– 29).

When I quoted this passage in response to a friend's concern about my financial well-being after I launched my protest leave without pay at Harvard, he said, "Yeah, Derrick, but you ain't no goddamn lily." We both laughed. Later, he invited me to give a lecture series that both lifted my spirits and helped me pay my bills. Good fortune of that character is welcome, but not guaranteed. It may ease but can't alter the reality that adherence to ethical standards requires turning away or placing at risk positions or advancements for which we have worked hard and to which we feel entitled. Doing so enables us to respond to the challenges of making our way in a society that boasts of color-blindness and equal opportunity, but adheres to myriad practices that provide what appear to be presumptions and preferences to whiteness, male gender, sexual straightness, physical normalcy, and brute economic power.

I truly believe that in making honorable choices about our lives, we can acknowledge sacrifices we make and the risks we take and recognize that what others view as losses and foolhardiness are the nourishment upon which our spirits thrive. I certainly know what I am giving up when I make those choices, but the sacrifice evolves into the courage to move forward even when my convictions conflict with my career goals. As others have done before me, as many are quietly doing now, I believe we can remain true to our convictions: We can choose ethics over advancement and never regret the choice.

Rather than mourn our losses, we can devote our minds and our time to finding a new path to our career goals that honors those convictions, even if that path seems longer and harder than the one we had hoped to take. There is a marvelous irony here. It is not guaranteed, but so often for me, as for others, the ethical path can prove the more effective and fulfilling route to success. Even when the ethical way leads to loss rather than gain, animosity rather than acclaim, there is reassurance in the knowledge that compromising my integrity would not have led me to an outcome that was meaningful and satisfying.

It is not, of course, a betrayal of ethical ambitions when circumstances require that you remain in a job or a relationship that is not evil, but not very rewarding. Duty to family, to children, to elderly parents, even to an employer may mandate remaining in a job with little future and even less satisfaction. In order to maintain their health coverage or for any number of reasons, likely millions of Americans — at every income level — find themselves trapped in unfulfilling jobs. Even in this situation, you will be faced with choices that can have a profound effect on your spirit. If you perform your job as well as you can, treat your co-workers with the respect they deserve, and, if the opportunity arises, stand up in some small way to a practice, policy, or environment that you see as demeaning or simply less than ideal, your job — even though it may not be the one you always dreamed of — can give you a measure of satisfaction.

I recognize that my statements of outreach seem in direct contradiction to what we see in the world, where the standard is taking rather than giving. Even so, I don't consider ethical ambition an oxymoron. Ethical conduct connotes activity that is fair, uplifting, in keeping with and, one hopes, advancing moral norms. Ambition is an earnest desire for some accomplishment or distinction and the willingness to strive for it. Usually, ambition is associated with those seeking success as measured by a desire for wealth, position, power, or celebrity. I have found, though, that even in our highly competitive society where the goal of making it to the top is more important than how we get there, an individual whose ambition is to live an ethical life can gain both an inner dignity and an overall serenity that money and position can't buy. And again, in strange and usually unpredictable ways, the ethically ambitious person, on occasion, can achieve impressive success as the society usually defines that term.

Diligent effort in support of good intentions is critical for those pursuing ethical ambition. The Epistle of James puts it well: "So faith by itself, if it has no works, is dead" (James 2:14). Ethical work often involves gleaning in the vineyard of injustice while trying to make things better. It is often difficult, unpopular, and unappreciated, but it can be self-sustaining. Persons working for social reform most often put in long hours and accept much smaller salaries than do those in big business. Their compensation is in the work itself.

This book addresses the paradox of success for those who genuinely want to live lives that matter. The obstacles to this goal, unless negotiated with a seemingly contradictory combination of integrity and guile, can undo persons of ability today as effectively as racial discrimination and rigid class barriers. Again, there is not an identifiable set of components that are essential to ethical functioning. I have chosen to explore six areas of importance to me: passion, courage, faith, relationships, inspiration, and humility.

There are certainly others, and surely there is overlap and interconnection with the areas I've outlined. Through these explorations, I hope to encourage those who long to live meaningful lives with dignity and integrity.

I want to highlight the benefits of making honorable choices; it lifts the spirit and relieves the pain of loss as we seek new routes, which though uncertain, may prove the shortest and most fulfilling routes to our goals. Following the publication of my book *Confronting Authority*, which reviewed the several jobs I have surrendered on what I hoped were principled reasons, I received an uplifting letter from a man who wrote that he had been working at a home for battered women, first as a volunteer and later as a member of the paid staff. He loved the work and felt he had found his calling. Then, new leaders came and set policies that he felt were unjust and contrary to the needs of the women served there. After registering his protests without success, he concluded reluctantly that he had to leave. He resigned with a heavy heart. He reported that he had a tough time for a while, but wanted me to know that eventually he found and joined another battered women's shelter that was better in every way. Making the hard ethical choice had led him to what he said by any measure was a more successful life.

A heartwarming story with a happy ending, but those who choose this path will often find that they are outsiders, rejected or misunderstood by those who believe that material success is everything, or those who fear changing their minds or their lives. The sense that you are an outsider can be an especially lonely enterprise because the longing for acceptance and approval is enormously powerful. We rarely acknowledge the magnetic pull of this longing once we pass the trials of adolescence, but it affects all of us throughout our lives. For this reason, one of the purposes of this book is to acknowledge and celebrate the difficulties of going one's way in opposition to the consensus. Having experienced the chill of rejection, I can offer support and critical companionship for those others who choose integrity over the cloying comfort of conformance. You can come to recognize that you are not an outsider, that your principled stance has propelled you to the center of a controversy, and that you are respected, if not admired.

My goal is to inspire and encourage people, whatever their color or status, to achieve their full potential while simultaneously affirming for them and with them that the road they travel to success is often filled with barriers. It is my desire to help prepare future "outsiders" for the difficulties they will face as they strive for success, whether those difficulties take the shape of insidious media images, firings, negative reviews, the absence of promotions, or outright rejection.

Rising to the challenge is what makes possible the revelation that humanity at its essence is both an ongoing readiness to recognize wrongs and try to make things better, and the desire to help those in need of assistance without expecting reward or public recognition. It is a difficult task, but no other endeavor better conveys the certainty that this is what life is about; this is why we are here.

CHAPTER ONE

THE POWER
IN PASSION

An ethical endeavor at which you can work
with passion and integrity is a key component
in a satisfying life.

W HEN MOST OF us hear the word "passion," we
connect it immediately with romantic love, and often
with romantic love gone awry. Novels, films, television, even
our newspapers, are filled with stories, some fictional, some all
too real, evidencing the power in romantic passion, love at its
most heated, headlong, and heedless. The very phrase
"Grand Opera," for example, evokes tales of passion savored,
betrayed, and lost, all in ravishing music. Consider Verdi's
Aïda: An enslaved Ethiopian princess and the commander of
the Egyptian army, despite the danger, fall in love, choose
their passion over allegiance to their countries, and sustain
that love even unto death.

Romantic passion can be marvelous and uplifting. It can
also be corrupting and destructive. But passion, of course,
covers territory far broader than romantic love. And I think

that an ethical life is, of necessity, a passionate one. Simply relying on a generalized hope to do good in life is a poor shield against the forces insisting that integrity and ethical behavior are necessary sacrifices on the road to success. The dominant cultural messages offer a seductive attraction to goals of income, fame, and status. After all, by definition, a capitalist society is one in which wealth is generated through harvesting as profit the work product of others. To become a successful player in this economic system, we are led to believe that success *demands* sacrifice: If it's worth anything, it's worth everything.

True success often does demand sacrifice, but not of virtue, not of our beliefs, not of our desires and moral goals, certainly not in the often futile and always empty pursuit of material success. Empty because wealth, status, and celebrity do not guarantee and often subvert a meaningful quality of life. Yes, we have before us constantly the titans of the corporate world who are rewarded handsomely for their willingness to exploit employees, shamelessly produce and promote products regardless of their quality or usefulness, all while engaging in ruthless practices intended to damage competitors. I cannot say that those responsible for such behavior lack passion in their work, but it is a passion that deserves far more condemnation than it receives. It is certainly not a passion that I would wish to emulate or espouse to those who come to me seeking advice on ethical ambition. And I am not impressed that corporate heads engaged in these and a myriad of other morally indefensible policies seek to sanitize them by boasting of their charitable giving and involvement in good causes.

Living in the midst of a culture of hypocrisy and legalized but no less damaging practices, it is understandable that the slippery road toward unethical behavior too often follows the conclusion that we can't pursue our heart's passion *and* adhere to ethical standards. Avoiding being drawn into this seemingly pragmatic posture requires a character of resistance that is enhanced by a passion for integrity rather than success. Adherence to that passion can be sacrificial, but it can also enable achievements that are more impressive than those attained by people who believe that there is no place for ethical passion in a hard-hearted world.

I know that many students are in law school not because the study and practice of law appeals to them, but because of social pressure or their hope for financial security and their expectation that law offers them a stable future. Even when these students are able to achieve academically and later professionally, there is no guarantee that they won't be dissatisfied, even miserable in the very profession they've sacrificed so much to enter. When they come to me for advice, I find myself saying, "You may be finding it difficult to decide whether the law is what you want as a profession, because you may not know who you want to *be*." And yet I feel a degree of hope for these students because they at least have the courage to admit their doubts.

After all, in choosing law school in the mid–1950s, I held similar hopes to those that attract my students. In addition, I nurtured the notion that I might use legal skills in the fight to end racial discrimination. Encouraged by the stature of the black lawyers I had met during high school and college, law seemed more promising than social work, teaching, preaching, medical school, or any other of the narrow range of work that appeared available to an ambitious black person in those days.

Early on, I wanted to be a writer. I enjoyed the challenge of conveying my thoughts into words. Unfortunately, whatever feeling I had for it was diluted by the lack of encouraging models and job opportunities. I envisioned starving in a cold-water flat, not an enticing prospect for a young black boy who had watched his parents work their way out of poverty. At that point, my interest in writing did not develop into a passion.

While sheltered from the most viciously destructive forms of racial segregation, I certainly was aware of them, hearing my family discuss them in tones of both rage and resignation. Over the years, I nurtured the feeling that I might do something to alter a racial landscape that appeared permanently fixed and immutable. The law I was told and slowly came to believe was an arena where I could put my strong feelings to work. Fresh from two years in the service, I entered law school determined to prepare myself to take part in the civil rights battles that lay ahead.

My passion for racial justice grew out of years of work in the field, first as a litigator and then administrator, and later as a teacher and a writer. I channeled my writing into legal briefs and motions in civil rights practice, and later into teaching and law review articles. A teaching position provided a platform for writing legal essays and then allegorical stories. Musing at length on the nature of passion, I realize that the fervor of my feelings about justice has motivated my entry into activities where my passion could take the form of writing.

Whatever one's area of endeavor, pursuing it with passion is not easy. As described earlier, our culture confuses the function of passion in our lives. We are pushed off course by the prejudices and imbalances of power with which we all must contend. It is essential that the ethical person acknowledge society's injustices and, whether or not called to ease them, recognize the disadvantaged, those who have been squeezed out unfairly despite the nation's boast that all here have an equal chance to gain a share of the nation's riches. For those determined to address these inequalities, despite the economic and political barriers, a passionate commitment is needed to support the belief that our actions can have a positive effect on those we are trying to help. Even for those whose lives do not revolve around working toward social reform and change, opportunities to choose for the good on a smaller scale can actually arise more often. The challenge for all of us is not to look at the ethical choice any given moment presents us with and too readily conclude, "Oh, that one's not important."

I understand, of course, that for many the journey to uncover and then affirm their heart's passion requires what may appear an endless search. This is particularly true for those of us who for whatever reason are deemed "outsiders," with no ready access to the mainstream of resources, contacts, and influence. Particularly for those in this group, I won't pretend that "finding your passion" is the key that will unlock the mysteries of all life's issues. That's not passion – that's magic, and as far as I know, it doesn't exist. I can say, though, that passion is an energy that already exists inside each of us.

It is well to recognize the stereotypes of passion we take for granted so that we can get clear on what passion is not. Countless things in our popular culture inculcate in us the idea that passion is the precious thing we feel only in life's climactic moments. In childhood, we may mistake "the passionate life" for swashbuckling adventure, or romantic intensity, if not both. For boys, stereotypically, it might be imagined in fantasies of daring escapes behind enemy lines, fierce gun battles, or winning the big game; for girls, just as stereotypically, it might be stolen kisses, accepting the Oscar for Best Actress, or being swept away by Mr Right. As we grow older our ideas about exultant moments of passion tend to get more specific if not more realistic: hitting the lottery, reaching the pinnacle of whatever career we've imagined for ourselves, reciprocated romance with the person of our desire. Television commercials aim to connect these moments with acquisition of the products they are promoting, alas with an alarming degree of success.

Even without televised assistance, the culturally connected passion always has a soundtrack that swells with crescendos. This passion comes so rarely that the rest of our life, aside from those precious moments, seems nothing but buildup and anticlimax – if moments like those happen for us at all. As we settle into the workaday realities of adulthood, we may come to believe that passion is something that happens to other people, and we settle for being spectators to passion. We consume it vicariously through movies, TV shows, sports, music videos, books, newspapers, magazines – any medium that can package intense life into morsels for us to swallow in our spare time.

But this idea of passion is, rather obviously, a perversion of genuine feeling. It looks at the spectrum of human emotion, takes one extreme, and elevates that extreme to the position of the greatest good. It's as if we surveyed the whole range of forms of physical intimacy between two people and determined that the only worthwhile part of it was orgasm; everything else, if we can't dispense with it altogether, is just something we have to tolerate until the next orgasm comes along. This is all wrong: Passion is not an event, but an energy; and it's an energy that exists in all of us, all the time. The question is not whether we have it but whether we access it, and how we channel it. But this energy is not limited to vocation, and has value beyond the oft-heard and not always wise advice to "do what you love."

Kenny Rogers, the country singer, said that his mother told him early on to find something he loved to do and he would never have to work a day in his life. In my experience, Rogers's mother was accurate for those who both know and can find what they love. Successful entertainers, particularly those who have been around for a number of years, usually have worked very hard to achieve fame and wealth. When they are interviewed, though, they inevitably report that they remain in the business because of their passion: performing and bringing joy to their audiences.

Joe Ligon, lead singer of the gospel group the Mighty Clouds of Joy, speaks of an interview with a reporter who asked him what was the most important thing that had happened in his thirty years singing with the group. The reporter suggested it might have been when the group sang in any of a number of foreign countries, or when they performed for the president of the United States. Joe Ligon shook his head. Then he recalled a night when they were getting ready to perform in Rochester, New York. A man came up, introduced himself, and said that he learned the group was in town and just had to thank him. He explained that, years ago, he was deeply depressed. He had lost first his wife and then his job and had children to support and no way to support them. Deep in despair, he went into his bedroom and got a gun, planning to kill his children and then himself. But he had heard the recordings of the Mighty Clouds of Joy and their music turned him around. He found God and is now back on his feet. Joe Ligon told the reporter, that man's story was the most important thing that happened in his career. In effect, Ligon's singing, his passion, was a ministry intended to move people toward understanding the value of life as this man had been moved.

In less "glamorous" occupations, and particularly in helping fields such as medicine, teaching, social work, and charitable operations, the story is usually the same. Whether well paid or not, the chief satisfactions are those that involve reaching out to others, trying to make things better. Again, I want to stress that passion for one's work is not limited to occupations that at least seem to be dedicated primarily to public good. I know many people who work in the private sector at jobs that have little or no apparent connection to the public weal, yet who bring to those jobs the same passion they bring to the rest of their lives. As a result, they do not have the artificial dividing line between Work and Life that so many of us experience, and they do not feel as if they have to turn their passion on and off like water from a tap. Those who develop a passion for their work gain pleasure from it, and are rewarded with satisfactions that can't be taken away.

That has certainly been my experience. After several years in civil rights litigation and administration to which I was entirely devoted, I sought a law teaching job because I felt it would provide me an opportunity to write and perhaps publish. It has certainly done that, but without doubt my efforts to share my life experiences with students utilizing the courses I teach and my writing as the vehicle have proven the most satisfying aspect of the job. Having students on graduation day tell me that my course was the most meaningful they had in their three years of law school is no less precious because there is nothing in the compliments I can deposit in a bank.

I am doing what I love, but I recognize that the exhortation to "do what you love" must, of necessity, compete with messages that we have to be realistic, choose security, and sacrifice what matters to us if we want to pay basic bills, to say nothing of getting ahead. And such messages have a pragmatic attraction not present when we are urged to find our passion, to do what we want and success will follow. For most, the latter sounds like pure fantasy and can, in fact, prove unrealistic for those in the performing arts where there is so much talent and so few jobs.

After my wife, Jewel, died, I asked Bill Cosby to speak to my actor son, Douglass, about returning to college and gaining another skill, perhaps teaching or social work. I thought that he should prepare himself to earn a living while continuing to seek a break in the tough acting field. Cosby, after all, is a successful actor and entertainer, but one quite proud of his Ph.D. in education. He agreed, and invited Douglass to his dressing room following a filming session. My son was ecstatic after the meeting. "What did he tell you?" I asked. "Well," Douglass replied, "after talking to me for some time he told me he understood me better than you, Dad. And he told me to follow my dream." Cosby had not said what I had hoped he would, but perhaps he was able from his distance to offer Douglass clearer and more useful guidance than I could from my proximity as Douglass's father.

For difficult but less competitive fields, the follow-your-dream admonition may seem to be more easily realized: a girl with a passion for healing becomes a doctor, a boy with a passion for justice becomes a lawyer. Gaining access to a field, though, even when passion is present, does not insulate one from the frustrations to effective service. Just because you're working as a doctor doesn't mean you're always healing — there's a lot about insurance companies and HMOs and hospital policies that doesn't involve and even can become a barrier to healing. Just because you're working as a lawyer — even in your dream job with a public interest firm whose primary work is for a cause you believe in — doesn't guarantee that you will be pursuing justice for your clients throughout the workday.

Whatever our passion, we encounter detours, roadblocks, collateral difficulties. The challenge is to get beyond these inevitable barriers. I recognized soon after I became a professor that I had a passion for teaching. While I had done satisfactory work as a litigator, I enjoyed my students but did not much enjoy the frustration of faculty meetings. It was not that I wished to shirk my share of administrative duties, but that my views and perspectives were often quite different from those of my faculty colleagues. Mine reflected my background, my experiences, which were poles away from those they held, yes, and held passionately.

In all too many faculty votes, I found myself on the dissenting side. What was more dispiriting was during faculty meetings, even when I made a point that seemed of value, it was not recognized until one of the men the faculty really respected said virtually the same thing. In subsequent discussion, it became this professor's point and was referred to in laudatory terms. This happens to all of us in meetings from time to time. It happened so often to me that I came to dread faculty meetings. Happily, after leaving Harvard, I joined the NYU Law School faculty as a permanent visitor. I teach and, thank goodness, I have no obligation to attend faculty meetings.

Passion without any sense of responsibility to others can be, in fact, irresponsible. Jussi Bjoerling, perhaps the greatest tenor of the twentieth century, after a lengthy absence from the Metropolitan Opera, told an acquaintance, "This is the place to be . . . colleagues from all over. Here you really find out." In other words, the greater the vocal company, the better he liked it. Asked why he didn't sing more opera at the Met, Bjoerling responded quickly, "Because I make more singing concerts, and I have to think of my family."[1] He was very clear on what his passion was, and just as clear that his responsibilities took priority. Trying to live exclusively for one's passion would be as irresponsible as trying to live exclusively for one's responsibilities, minus passion.

Let me share with you a story about an instance when I allowed an ethical passion to lead me astray because I did not temper it with responsibility. It happened at a time when I was younger and less able to differentiate the passion for personal affirmation from my larger passion for social justice. Though the experience was mine, it was a lesson I learned from Thurgood Marshall.

On a bitterly cold day back in 1961, I had taken a flight across the South, headed for Jackson, Mississippi, but a blizzard there forced the plane down in Memphis, Tennessee. Passengers were told to line up to get hotel reservations. I don't remember where the white passengers were assigned, but I was dropped by the airline bus at a black motel, the Lorraine, later to gain notoriety as the place where Dr Martin Luther King was killed. It was late and the sleepy motel desk clerk assigned me to a room that had not been cleaned since its apparent earlier use by some of the motel's "transient trade." I decided to make the best of it, but unfortunately the room was also unheated. After an hour or so of discomfort, I decided to take one of the other options offered at the airport – a late train to Jackson. I checked out and walked with my bags three or four blocks down the middle of snow-filled streets to the train station.

Arriving in Jackson, cold and tired after an uncomfortable several hours on the crowded, unheated train, I went into the waiting room to call Jack Young, one of only three black lawyers in the state, to ask him to pick me up. Before I could place the call, two very large, white policemen banged on the booth and ordered me out. Only then did I realize that I was in the white waiting room. Nonetheless, my anger overcoming appropriate prudence, I explained why I was using the phone, and tried to complete my call. The policemen paid no attention, continuing to order me out. Before I could reach Jack Young, they dragged me out of the telephone booth and placed me under arrest. On the way to what I hoped was the police station, but suddenly feared could be my last ride to nowhere, I realized that my rage had placed me in a vulnerable position. I was fearful for my safety, but proud of the passion that demanded respect even in a hostile environment. I imagine any number of civil rights activists have experienced quite similar feelings. When the police car stopped, it was in front of the city jail. After processing, I spent the night in a holding cell with several other men. None were, like me, wearing a suit and tie, but no one bothered me.

The next morning, Jack Young bailed me out, and at my hearing asked the local judge to file the charges. The judge did so after lecturing me at length on the need to obey local laws. The Supreme Court had declared segregation laws unconstitutional years before, but I decided not to remind the judge of rulings he surely knew as well as I. When I returned to New York, I got another lecture from Thurgood Marshall. "Damn, boy, the black folks down South need good lawyering. They don't need dead heroes. They got plenty of them already. Understand? Do your protesting in the courtroom, not in the railroad station."

Thurgood Marshall had gone to the South any number of times in the 1940s and 1950s when it was really dangerous. He once recalled getting off a train in a small town to represent a black man accused of raping a white woman. The atmosphere was tense and the hostility of whites as he left the train was all too obvious.

"How did you handle the situation?" I asked him.

"First thing I did," Thurgood said, "was take my civil rights out, fold them carefully, and stick them way, way down at the bottom of my hip pocket. *And*," he added dramatically – he loved telling stories – "I *left* them there until I finished the case and got back on that train, hauling ass out of there!"

I tell this story to show how even passion that seems ethical and just must be leavened with common sense. Marshall's message was clear: No one expects you to challenge hostile individuals, particularly when doing so will almost certainly result in bodily harm to you or others. This standard, of course, is sometimes easier to state than it is to apply in the heat of the moment. Recognizing those situations and making appropriate decisions is a necessary caveat even for those of us committed passionately to ethical investments.

Unfortunately, for the many who are not able to act on the "do what you love" message, "passion" can become a Holy Grail, the unattainable ideal: "Well, my passion is acting, but that doesn't pay the rent, so here I am . . ."; "Painting is my real passion, but I realized I had to find a career, so . . ." If you think of passion in terms of desire, and not energy, if you see passion as all about *want* and *lack*, and somebody asks you what you're passionate about, your answer might invalidate 90 per cent of the life you're living. If, for example, you think of your job as the thing you have to do to pay the rent or the mortgage and put food on the table, you undermine the possibility of living passionately almost from the moment you wake up. As I understand it, cognitive behavior psychology suggests that our thoughts – specifically our thought processes – shape our emotions at least as much as vice versa, and that we can, in effect, often work consciously (as well as subconsciously) toward a particular state of mind. Just as we can convince ourselves through unspoken internal choruses that things are headed for the worst when we really can't know the outcome of a particular situation ("This'll never work, I'm a failure, what's the point in trying . . ."), we can use the same practices to focus our energies into passion.

The reality is that your passion *might* be compatible or even complementary with your vocation. If we feel that our passion draws us to a specific career, it's not the career itself we're drawn to but an energy we think we'll tap into *through* that career. The label (doctor, lawyer, singer, teacher, accountant, secretary, actor . . .) is just shorthand for the energy we're drawn toward. What we're really saying is that we love how we *feel* when we engage in that thing. And this is where it starts to become clear how passion can be an electrical current, an endless energy. In essence, passion can be the fuel that powers the ethical engine. An ethical life is usually also a passionate life.

I guess I just lack passion. We have all heard or said this before. *Maybe I just don't have the passion you have.* If you feel that way yourself, you may be wondering how I can still argue that there is passion in all of us, all of the time. What I call passion is the energy that courses within us and through us as long as we're alive. As we have discussed earlier, it is inherently neither good nor bad; it's the purpose you put it to that determines its value.

You've surely felt a heady rush of positive energy at certain times in your life. It could have been a public experience, such as singing in a choir, acting in a play, scoring in a game, winning a contest, making a speech, receiving an award or a diploma; or a private one, such as solving a knotty problem, fixing something that was broken, having a meeting of minds with someone, feeling the presence of God, realizing that someone you care for also cares for you. You felt the power of it, and the power felt good.

Chances are you've felt a rush of energy for less-positive reasons too: Maybe you got the last word in an argument because winning felt more important than finding common ground, or you took full credit for something you'd only helped with, or you got pleasure hearing about someone else's misfortune, or you even just decided not to make the effort to do something that would help you (exercise, get sufficient sleep, give up smoking) because you thought, *Who's it hurting?* or *Who'll know?* These two energies can be called nourishing passion and denying passion, respectively.

The difference between a passion that nourishes and one that denies you is that the first enhances the experience of being present, and the second facilitates the experience of escape. So contrary to popular belief, passion is not something you have or you don't, or that has to be fed or it dies. It's something that grows strong because you nourish it with the experiential equivalent of healthy food and sunlight, or wastes away because you deny it the attention and nourishment it needs to thrive.

Passion will respond to the buzz of a quick fix: sarcasm, too much junk food, impulse buying, gossip, rage . . . But it thrives on substance: a job well done, giving credit to others, standing up for what you believe in, voluntarily returning lost valuables, choosing what feels right over what might feel good right now. In other words, nourishing passion is ethical passion — it's finding power in doing the right thing.

I decided to begin this book with a meditation on passion because I think it is crucial to a meaningful life, especially for those on the margins. Even when we are not materially deprived, we often live with a gnawing fear that our hold on what we have is tenuous. Lord knows, I certainly live with a sense that what I have or have achieved — materially, professionally, or in personal happiness — can be snatched away from me at any time. Surprisingly, I find this concern both scary and strangely liberating, providing a kind of "what the hell" willingness to choose the good over the safe when the two are not the same.

This may seem foolish, but it strengthens passion, especially for the already marginalized. The sacrifice of passion is a kind of psychic suicide. The playing field is not level, but no one — even those in whose favor the field tilts — can control how much passion we bring to the game, and how much pleasure we take from it. In the hands of outsiders, passion transforms failure and creates ethical autonomy. If you hold fast to your passion, you can't be a slave to someone else's game or agenda. That doesn't mean you can't achieve within traditional structures, but passion can protect you within those structures as well as give you the courage to create your own — either within the existing parameters or striking new ground.

I hope I haven't made it seem that you can one day decide

to live ethically and that from that point on your choices become clear – with the *right* choice in any situation flashing its neon sign. Nothing could be further from the truth. The decision to live ethically is no more effective than most New Year's resolutions. Living ethically is a process, a habit that must be refreshed frequently. That's what this book is about – the process you go through to assess your situations and learn from your choices so that as each new situation arises, the inclination to choose ethically is stronger in you, even if the right path is less than clear. What you can do right away is ask yourself questions like these: Are my goals worthwhile and important? Am I living in a way that helps me achieve those goals responsibly? Morally? These are questions we should be asking ourselves daily, not just on New Year's and birthdays.

Having set down these thoughts on passion and its ethical power, I am wary of giving what might be thought of as pat answers and glib advice. The road to ethical passion is unique to each individual. What I hope to have accomplished with this chapter is to provide a meditation, a space of reflection and thoughtful contemplation. I hope it provides a sense that you need not check your passion at the door to succeed. Your passion, whatever your calling, profession, or job, is the key to your pleasure in life, the seat of your power, and the root of your sense of agency in the world.

It is my most ardent hope that by helping people under-stand that their passion is already present in them, they will awaken to what is passionate for them in their lives. In so doing, they can realize that they don't have to buy into the false dichotomies of passion versus success, of integrity versus success, of ethical living versus success, of virtue versus success. Success in the ethical sense is possible right here and right now, no matter who you are and what you're doing. If you wake up and feel strongly, passionately about one or several aspects of your life, you are already on the road to the only success that really matters.

CHAPTER TWO

COURAGE AND RISK TAKING

*Ethical living is an ongoing commitment, as we
meet life's day-to-day challenges and opportunities,
to assume risks in honor of self and all others.*

Courage

NUMEROUS TIMES IN my life I have been called
"courageous." This sounds like a worthy thing, but
popular culture uses the word so often and so glibly that the
meaning of courage is obscured. In this chapter I want to
sort out what courage might really mean when used to
describe a life that aspires through ethical action toward
ethical goals. To begin with, there can be no courage
without a context. More to the point, it is impossible to
have any meaningful consideration of courage without also
considering the meaning and role of fear in our life.

As with most words that become catch-all compliments,
it is difficult to come up with a snap definition of "courage,"
although I can readily call up familiar images that evoke the

idea: the firefighter carrying the baby out of the burning building, adults on a sinking ship filling the last lifeboats with children and the infirm, soldiers going into a battle knowing they face almost certain defeat. Images such as these are universal in their ability to summon assumptions about both what's at risk and the degree to which the action is being taken in the face of that risk for a good beyond oneself.

This good, which extends far beyond a personal risk to yourself, is exemplified by a woman fighting to keep an abortion clinic open despite hostile phone threats at her home and loud and threatening protests mounted daily outside the clinic's front door. If, however, an action is taken in the face of great risk for a consequence that benefits you alone (you paddle a small boat through shark-infested waters to retrieve the Rolex that fell off your wrist while you were parasailing), we might be less inclined to call it courage; we might be moved to say, "Wow, that took guts," but probably no more than that (except, very possibly, "Wow, that was stupid.") As a general rule, we usually associate actions we call courageous with bravery, that is, taking an action despite known negative consequences, whether potential or guaranteed, and doing so selflessly, with greater concern for the good of another or others than for oneself. All of this understanding rests on a foundation of fear.

All too often in our society where "looking out for number one" has become the unspoken motto, ethical action usually requires courage that in turn requires overcoming fear. Influenced by the staged heroics of stars in adventure films, many people equate courage with fearlessness. Shakespeare had his Julius Caesar say, "Cowards die many times before their deaths; The valiant never taste of death but once" (II.ii). Wonderful lines, but in the real world if we don't fear the consequence of our action, what makes us brave or courageous for taking it? In fact, courage has no meaning if there is no consequence to be feared. The consequence feared might be minor ("If I say what I think, he'll be angry . . ."), but it must be real. You can feel at risk because your sense of self is threatened, or your job, or your ego, or the happiness of a loved one. The consequence might even seem of little importance to somebody else ("So they don't promote you, so you'll go work somewhere else, big deal"), but the consequence must seem real to you.

On the face of it, this may make the opportunity to be courageous sound as if it must be rare. "Well, I don't get in many dangerous situations, so I guess I won't have many chances to be brave . . ." This belief points up a common yet unspoken truth, the degree to which fear is a daily presence in our lives – and how much of what looks like daily life choices are all too frequently reactions to fear. To be human is to be brought up against fears, large and small, whether we're conscious of them or not.

Theologian Paul Tillich tells us that, unlike animals, we human beings are aware of our existence and its finite nature. This awareness is basic to our humanity: Anxiety grows out of it, and we early on adopted mechanisms to cope with anxiety and fears so severe that functioning would be otherwise impossible. There was a tremendous need for some sense of stability and meaning in a world that was otherwise meaningless and all too transitory. For many, belief in an all-knowing, all-powerful God served that function. Life was still scary, but anxiety and fear became manageable in the context of the knowledge that Someone Up There was in charge.[2]

Tillich also addresses the fundamental question of life's meaning and purpose for those for whom scientific knowledge prevents a belief in an all-knowing deity. It is possible, he argues, for everyone to invoke a "courage of confidence" under which genuine belief can be sustained despite circumstances tending to destroy it.

Rev. Peter J. Gomes explains that this courage of confidence is nurtured when we are able to "believe in love in the face of hatred, life in the face of death, day in the dark of night, good in the face of evil . . ."[3] For Tillich, these are all manifestations of enormous courage, the courage of confidence in more than the sovereignty of fact and appearance.

I take two points from Tillich here: The first is that we all have the opportunity to face fear, but that would be small consolation without the second; the second is that the single most effective tool we've been given to work with our fear is courage. Contrary to Shakespeare's Caesar, courage is not a quality you have or don't have; nobody is born courageous, nobody has courage all the time, and nobody who has not yet been courageous lacks the possibility of choosing it in the future. Courage is a decision you make to act in a way that works through your own fear for the greater good as opposed to pure self-interest. Courage means putting at risk your immediate self-interest for what you believe is right. The stakes don't have to be life and death, and the situation doesn't have to be dramatic. You could exercise courage in a conversation where the greatest risk you run is being yelled at, laughed at, or refused. When concerned white students ask what they might do as individuals to challenge racist views, I suggest that they might well start with their families and friends. Based on what some of them have told me about the racial views held by many of their family members and friends, speaking out will take real courage.

This example illustrates why I distrust the unexamined use of the word "courage" to describe my life or others': By itself, it diminishes the ethical motivation underlying the action. Courage is our tool in vanquishing fear, but it's not always an easy tool to use, and truth be told, it's rarely glamorous. It's a daily decision to wake up and try to do the right thing, no matter how big the reward or how great the fear.

Courage is not monolithic – there are probably as many different varieties of it as there are of fear. For the purposes of thinking about how it relates to living ethically, I find it helpful to think of courage in three categories: personal, group, and the courage of your convictions.

Personal courage is not always a thought-out decision. It can arise from purely internal perceptions ("I have to prove myself!") or from external causes that are physical ("I'm really hurting, but forty more yards and I'll have set a school record"). The situation might be job-related: "I hear the boss is thinking of passing you over for promotion. What are you going to do?" While your response may require some bravery, what you're defending is purely personal. Courage, on the other hand, although frequently sparked by personal things, requires more than simply a brave response. It requires making a morally inflected decision. The story that follows details the very first time I began thinking for myself about acting ethically even in the face of a threat. That said, it's not a story of fully evolved courage because the stand I took was simply in my own interest. But the indignation I felt for myself would later mature into an indignation for others who might be taken advantage of.

When I was eleven and began delivering the *Pittsburgh Press*, a big challenge was avoiding the neighborhood bully, Lucky Babs. When I did run into him, he would "ask" me for money in a tone that implied "or else." Without even pretending to protest, I would reach into my pocket and gave him a dime or a quarter – a goodly percentage of what I earned each day.

I wasn't happy with my behavior, but I rationalized it.

Even at age eleven I was sure I had a future, and equally sure that guys like Lucky Babs did not. They were tough enough, but they came from difficult home situations, and were always in trouble in school, if they even bothered showing up at all. Let them have their few pennies of protection money, I told myself. It's better to pay than get beaten up, maybe even really hurt.

But one day I got tired of making long detours to avoid Lucky. Going way out of my way usually kept me from having to pay, and having to pay kept me from getting beaten up, but they were both doing serious damage to my sense of self. I knew a showdown was inevitable, and it came quickly. I was on my route, passing through Lucky's turf, and sure enough there he was, asking for a dime – or else.

"Lucky," I told him as calmly as my shaking voice permitted, "I know you're bigger than me, and you can fight better than I can, but I'm not giving you any more money. You'll have to beat me first." I didn't strike a fighting pose – I didn't have any. Lucky gave me a long, quizzical look, then laughed and gave me a hard punch on the arm.

"Hell, man, I don't need your damn money." He never hassled me again.

The incident taught me that just because I was afraid and lacked power or authority, I didn't have to shy away from confrontation with those who were trying to intimidate me. The fear of standing up for yourself is always more likely to keep you in a position of subordination than the thing you fear itself. Over time, I learned that directly confronting the scary things in life let me both acknowledge my fear and move through it to appropriate action.

What I call group courage is the kind that's called for when you're specifically targeted because you're part of a group, whether it's because of your race, sex, affiliation, neighborhood, or nationality. It is personal courage in the service of the group. Those targeting you don't care about who you are personally, what you do in your spare time, what you like or dislike – in all likelihood you are merely a symbol to those attacking your larger group, which means that your humanity probably doesn't even enter into the equation. The classic instance of group courage is the courage of soldiers, and I draw my example from my stint in Korea.

Courage is not necessarily heroism, and I was nothing like a hero during my year in Korea, but I did have plenty of exposure to fear, and that gave me plenty of chances to meet fear with courage.

By the time of the signing of the armistice on July 27, 1953, the Korean War had lasted almost three years and had taken the lives of some four million people, forty thousand of them American service members. Two fifths of South Korea's industrial facilities were destroyed, along with a third of its homes. The country was totally devastated by the war. On my trips to Seoul and the countryside around the base, I don't think I ever saw a standing tree or an undamaged structure. Nothing seemed to escape the war's destruction. This almost lunar landscape was what greeted me my first day in the country; the first night I was greeted by an air raid. It was a greeting repeated frequently in the first weeks of my year-long "tour," and yet that was not the most frightening part of the year. That dubious honor fell to my biweekly turn as officer of the guard.

The duty was simple: I had to walk the perimeter of the base twice during the night, checking on the airmen standing guard at a dozen or so widely spaced guard posts. I carried a .45 automatic with which, in a brief training session, I revealed an amazing incompetence in proportion to my distrust of guns. The perimeter guards, all of them nineteen- and twenty-year-old airmen whose regular duties were maintenance or supply, seemed to know little more about their weapons than I did about mine. We would have been a sorry first line of defense if any enemy soldiers had managed to get behind our lines and attack the base.

But I wasn't really frightened of the designated enemy. Instead, my constant worry was that one of the young guards would get nervous and forget the password with which I responded to his "Who goes there?" So listening for a response at each of the dozen or so guard points was like waiting for a firing squad. I carried a flashlight that itself posed a tough choice. To use it made me a target for any enemy soldiers lurking near the perimeter fence. Not to use it meant I might frighten the guards into shooting first and then asking for the password later. Weighing the risks, I usually used my flashlight.

But the source of greatest fear was my imagination. I envisioned all manner of scenarios in which there was shouting, shooting, and general chaos. I did not survive in any of these imagined episodes. I could never decide whether putting my possessions in order before leaving my room for those guard tours constituted a jinx or simple prudence.

In retrospect, the real danger was comparatively small. It was the imagined dangers, with their resulting anxiety and fear, that I had to learn to live with to complete my tour of duty. I was part of a group of men whose safety – ultimately, whose lives – were in one another's hands. No matter how great my fear, I always knew that we each maintained the line within us. To give in to fear imperiled not only my own life, but the lives of my fellow soldiers. The experience prepared me well for my years doing civil rights law in the Deep South. And the physical dangers I faced there gave me confidence and strength when I entered uncharted territory, as I did when I began teaching law, a racial pioneer with almost none of the credentials generally thought essential. But however much we learn from our experiences, there is no graduation from fear training, no degree in courage. It is behavior that we must carry on for a lifetime.

Combining both personal and group courage means having "the courage of your convictions" – making your public actions correspond to your private beliefs. When you believe strongly in something, you are almost invariably challenged to put those beliefs to the test. In some ways this can be the least "dramatic" type of courage, but also the most inspiring, because while certain sacrifices may be absolutely logical for those who choose to make them, they never become easy. The vast majority of instances of this brand of courage go unreported, but examples are not hard to find.

In January of 2002, fifty officers and soldiers in reserve combat units of the Israeli Defense Forces signed a petition saying they refused to serve in the West Bank and Gaza Strip. The petition said in part: "The price of occupation is the loss of the Israel Defense Forces' semblance of humanity and the corruption of all of Israeli society. We will no longer fight beyond the Green Line [the pre-1967 boundary between Israel and the West Bank and the Gaza Strip] with the aim of dominating, expelling, starving, and humiliating an entire people." Within days there were over 150 signatures. The Israeli government warned in response that the signers could face disciplinary action, including prison.[4] One general characterized the protest as "incitement to rebellion," a charge on the order of treason.[5] These soldiers and officers manifested the courage of their convictions, placing conscience over military orders, a court-martial offense.

What was the source of their strength to do what they thought was right in the sure knowledge that their action would result in hostile reactions by their superiors, comrades in arms, and much of the country? It has to have been their beliefs in concerns greater than their own comfort, their own success, even their own freedom. And they might well have been inspired by what has become something of a tradition of principled protest in their ranks: Protests by serving members of the military brought down Prime Minister Golda Meir in 1973, created the Peace Now movement in 1978, led to the investigation of the massacre of Palestinians in Beirut's Sabra and Chatila refugee camps by Lebanese Christian militia who were allies of the Israeli Defense Forces, and ultimately the resignation of the then defense minister, Ariel Sharon. It is worth remembering when we make our own principled stands that each – whether or not successful – can be an example for the next.

I find that people trying hard to lead ethical lives must draw on courage frequently because standing up requires taking risks on a regular basis. In fact, risk taking is probably the most defining act of an ethical life. Ethics require us to think deeply about our positions on issues, and to take principled stands as a result of those positions. Principled stands will be tested regularly by a society that valorizes external indicators of success such as money and corporate power over much else. By understanding that courage is not a reflex, but a consequence of knowing your own mind, determining right and wrong for yourself and acting on that understanding, you create the possibility of risk taking in the interest of the greater good. Your good and the greater good become almost synonymous.

This clarity of thought, feeling, and action has resulted in some of our most powerful resistance: the war against fascism in World War II, the ending of the Vietnam War, the Velvet Revolution in Czechoslovakia, the fall of the Berlin Wall. Risk taking is a part of life whether one is ethical or not, but this is precisely why I feel it is so important to strive to become ethical. Only when we make a decision to live ethical lives, to aspire ethically, can we transform fear and our reactions to it into the reasoned resistance to the greed and exploitation that serve as a major barrier to a truly democratic society. Each ethical action represents an ongoing commitment as we meet life's day-to-day challenges and opportunities, a readiness to assume risks in honor of self and all others.

The Risk in Being

Some years ago, a television commercial opened with a very angry car company sales executive chewing out his obviously intimidated sales force. Dressed uniformly in dark suits and white shirts, they sit before him on straight-backed chairs. "I don't simply tell you that our competitor is doing better than we are in the year-end sales race," he bellows. "I blame you!"

A meek salesman stands and says in a tremulous voice, "Sir, if we built cars as well as our competitor, we would be selling as many cars as they are." Turning to his sales buddies for confirmation, he asks, "Isn't that right, guys?" Petrified, they don't move.

The commercial shifts to an enthusiastic description of the competitor's cars, then in the last few seconds, back to the angry sales exec, who growls, "Any more questions?" The camera pans across the sales force, still shaking in their seats, except for the one salesman who dared disagree with his boss. His chair is empty.

Now this was not a real-life incident, a moral tale, or even a moment in a larger narrative, like a movie; it was propaganda — a commercial designed to convince people to select and buy one make of car over another. But let us redeploy the propaganda for our own purposes and see how we might imagine it as a real-life situation, and make it work as a moral tale.

To begin with, why did the one lone salesman speak up in the first place? He wasn't a "hero type"; he was a skinny, nervous man who didn't look like he had the courage to challenge a soul. He had to know that this boss was in no mood to hear an underling concede the superiority of the competition's cars. Perhaps he hoped that the other sales-men, whom we can imagine complaining bitterly in private about the inferior quality of the cars they sold, would support his assertion in their boss's presence. If so, he was sorely disappointed, because the others chose instead to accept personal blame for poor sales figures that were likely the result of the product's shortcomings. That was the price they paid to keep their jobs. After sacrificing their own dignity, it would have been easy to abandon the one person with the courage to voice their views when it counted; to counter their own shame, it might even have felt necessary to let the single voice of truth twist in the wind.

I saw the commercial many times and still find it compelling because, in a painfully humorous way, it told the story of my life. It reflects the lives of many people who have spoken out with what they viewed as truth or right, even when the consequences of asserting those views might prove futile, or even dire. At first glance or even on careful review, these unhappy consequences are reasons for remaining silent – "you go along to get along." So, again, why did the lone salesman stand up and speak his mind knowing he could almost certainly expect the wrath of his boss and abandonment by his fellow workers? I have been where he was and done what he did, and while it felt right, it never felt easy.

Like the salesman, I am not confrontational by nature. To the contrary, I generally try hard to get along with people. After all, good relationships are comforting; hostility saps energy. Tensions in the workplace are unpleasant and render the job more difficult. And yet, on almost every job I have held – and there have been many – issues have arisen that led me to differ with my superiors. When I differed with them, it was less out of anger than because it hurt when, in my view, their actions were misguided, or unfair to me and to others. I don't rise to confront every discriminatory policy or practice – but sometimes, and an individual knows when they occur, the hurt is going to simmer, slowly doing harm deep down. What is the corrective to this, if not a cure? Protest the action, speak out against the policy, openly criticize the practice.

In short, I speak out to honor myself and those whose words or actions I am protesting. By remaining silent in the face of wrong or misguided behavior, I compound the wrong to myself by allowing the person I think is wrong to assume that his authority has vested him with an accurate sense of the situation. Challenging that embodies my duty to myself, to the person in authority, and to those in my group who have decided not to join me. This is so even when, as we can assume in the universe of the car commercial, the person speaking out is summarily dismissed. He has done his duty to himself and to others. The impact of his risk taking, though, will remain long after he has gone.

Imagine if, rather than lashing out, the sales exec had listened to the one man who had a different explanation of the company's poor sales record. Perhaps the others would have then felt they could suggest their views in a give-and-take discussion that might have produced a new sales plan designed to make the best of a bad situation. But in an environment where dominance sets the tone and substance of discourse, where it engenders fear all down the line, this kind of communication is very unlikely.

If you've ever been in a situation where you tried to offer useful information to a higher-up and got slapped down for your trouble, or tried to work with your colleagues to achieve a structural change in the organization and found that they were content to complain about the situation without fixing it, you probably think my "imagine if" is utopian at best. Superiors, often under pressure themselves, usually hear criticism as insubordination, and they tend to resist it by retaliating one way or another. And those in charge are hardly less annoyed than co-workers, who often view such challenges as senseless boat rocking, grandstanding, or both. Some co-workers might say, "Why didn't you check with us first? We could have talked it out, come to a consensus, and then presented a united front to the boss!"

I have heard this response more than a few times. I would have loved to have had allies in some of my early challenges to authority, but my efforts to change grouch sessions into forums for planning positive action were rarely successful. According to my co-workers, the time or the plan or the circumstances were never right. At the same time they felt uncomfortable about making excuses for not being candid with those in authority, and I was embarrassed by their efforts to rationalize inaction. After enough disappointments of this kind I stopped trying to organize and started speaking up or protesting on my own. Did I have less to lose than anyone else? Was I unaware of the risks I ran? No, on both counts: I had as much to lose as anyone, I was fully conscious of the risks I ran, and yet I chose to speak out. I did this despite the risks and despite the almost certain rejection (or worse, trivialization) of my concerns. I did it because I am committed to a cause that matters more to me than my own comfort, even (though I would never intentionally do anything to endanger them) more than the comfort of my loved ones. And if anything made it easier, it's the fact that it was something I practiced.

Even when a policy I protested did not personally affect me, I deemed its adoption or implementation an affront to everyone involved. I was part of the organization and, though I dissented from the policy's adoption, I felt responsible, as if the policy were being enacted in my name. Sometimes I was angry at those in power, but it was not anger or vengeance that motivated my speaking out or taking action. In a sense, it was fear: I was genuinely afraid that my tacit acquiescence to decisions I thought wrong would undermine my willingness to risk criticism, alienation, and serious loss to do what I thought right.

If my response to unjust behavior isn't unique to me, or extraordinary in some way, but perfectly reasonable, why you may ask do so few people confront those in authority?

Obvious answers come to mind: They have good sense; they need their jobs; they want to be team players, not troublemakers. Even on matters of relatively small importance, most people so fear opposing those in authority that they readily concede their rights and negate their best sense of themselves. I certainly do not condemn people who feel this way: In most cases, compliance with authority is not evil, and those in leadership positions are entitled to some respect in their decision-making role. More likely, though, those who remain silent simply don't want to be tarred with a label like "rabble-rouser," "troublemaker," or "whistle-blower." Neither did I. And yet when I disagreed strongly with certain actions – not all by any means – I became convinced that speaking out or mounting a protest was more important than "playing it safe."

Let's return for a moment to this notion of "practice." Most of the things we do habitually, for good or bad, are not the result of compulsion or addiction, but simply practice: You get up at 6:00 A.M. every day and go for your run; you check the alarm clock just before you turn off the lights; you brush your teeth twice each day. At some point you must have made a conscious decision to do these things, but eventually the actions became engrained – it would now take a conscious decision for you not to do them. We can just as easily accustom ourselves to habits of mind: switching to rage when we feel frustration; escaping into fantasy when we're overwhelmed; blaming others out of fear. But habits can be unlearned as well – good exchanged for bad, or bad for good. In the same way, we can make a habit, one choice at a time, of choosing the ethical, even when to do so means to risk. But before you start thinking that this sounds like a prescription for castor oil ("Yes, it's nasty all right, but it's so good for you!"), I'll let you in on a little secret: Choosing the good and doing good feels good.

I find again and again that there is an inherent sense of rightness in speaking one's mind in crucial situations. Doing so may well be scary (after all, it's not courage if there's not fear), but many people I've talked with describe feeling a kind of energy boost, perhaps an adrenaline rush, when they take up a challenge in a situation where all the chips are stacked on the other side. I have experienced this countless times, and I consider taking a risk in such circumstances an essential part of the life I choose to live each day.

When we contemplate the ways that people seek thrills, is it possible that we all need this feeling in one form or another, and that many who would not dare to challenge those in authority seek the needed assertion of self in the artificial thrill of playing the lottery, bungee jumping, or driving too fast? If it is possible, then it is sad to think how many people miss the more real and more humane thrill that can come when we stand up for what we believe is right against those we believe are wrong.

★   ★   ★

I would like to think that I have not given you the impression that I see all risks as equal, and all risks as worth taking – that I enjoy taking risk for the sheer fun of it. Like most people and objects, I tend toward inertia; I would generally rather not be at the heart of a conflict, and I only put myself there when I feel I must. But I do not leap to take every risk that comes along. I have not taken it upon myself to catalogue the varieties of risk, but let us assume that there are probably as many as there are types of courage.

One afternoon my sister Jan called me from Pittsburgh to report that the new management in her apartment building had announced an immediate rent increase of more than 30 per cent. Jan was furious, and so were the other tenants she had talked to. Together, she and I prepared a short petition complaining about the sudden increase and asking the management for a meeting. A united front, we felt, would bring the new management to its senses. Perhaps it would have, but my sister called back after spending more than two hours walking the halls and knocking on doors. The only signature on the petition was her own.

"I have heard every excuse in the book," she told me. "They all want to complain to me about the rent increase, but no one wants to challenge the landlord." Several did not answer their doorbell even though she knew they were home. One tenant told her angrily, "To hell with them. I'll just move out." Undaunted, my sister wrote letters to the new management, met with them, negotiated, and finally ended up with a much smaller rent increase. Jan was overjoyed, but it wasn't the first time she'd had the satisfaction of seeing that you can fight City Hall. She had twice taken the Chrysler Corporation to Small Claims Court to compel the company to make repairs on her car that she maintained were covered by her warranty. With time and effort, she prevailed in both cases. More of us might be willing to fight as my sister does if happy outcomes received the attention they deserve.

If so few of us are willing to rise to the challenge of an injustice as personally costly as an unfair rent hike, what would it take to get someone to rise to something far greater? As sad proof that righteous protest could have benefited both sides, months after my sister failed to enlist tenants to protest the rent increase, a substantial number moved out and have not been replaced; the building's management found itself in far worse financial shape than it had been prior to the increase that proved as unwise as it was unethical.

Taking action when you are treated unfairly has risks, but remaining silent can also be costly, to the spirit as well as to the pocketbook. Most of those who refused to sign my sister's petition were white and middle-class. They are likely paying more rent, or have moved to less desirable dwellings. Social reform workers are well aware of the pressures for compliance on people of color, on women, on gay men and lesbians of any color, and on those in nonmainstream religions. As my sister discovered, there are pressures to conform on those who are white and well-to-do. Whatever your race or status, though, failing to challenge unfair judgments or other forms of economic discrimination poses a continuing threat to both well-being and self-esteem. Avoiding confrontation by submitting to unfair treatment sets an unhealthy precedent for those seeking an ethically satisfying life.

Recognition of the risk of being ethical, of course, can come at a time of genuine crisis when the challenge to one's integrity becomes undeniable. Theologian Howard Thurman tells of a friend, a teacher in a divinity school, who for the first time in his life had to take a formal stand. The teacher's faculty was split over an important issue involving one of his colleagues and students – almost certainly a controversial faculty tenure or student grading issue, two of the few matters that rile an academic community. The political stakes were raised when the school's board of trustees became involved. The debate escalated and eventually all members of the faculty had to take a position for or against the position taken by the trustees.

Thurman's friend realized that his career and security were on the line, but his convictions put him on the side of the minority and against the trustees. He voted his convictions and the next fall, of necessity, he was teaching at another school. His decision cost him a job, but gained him an ethical triumph. In commenting on the situation he said: "For the first time in my life, I felt that I was a man. It was the first time that I could not hedge, but instead I had to take sides in accordance with the integrity of my convictions without regard to possible consequences. I became a new person, way down deep."[6]

Alice Walker, the writer and activist, would understand. She lived next door to us in Cambridge when she was a young writer, and one day told me a story that I have never forgotten. She had received a commission from a prestigious national magazine to write an article about growing up in the South. The exposure would have been valuable, as would the money. She was pleased with the article she wrote, but the magazine wanted her to make major changes.

Alice considered the changes worse than misguided; they were a violation of her integrity as a writer and a person, and she said so. But they were adamant. "Alice, you don't understand. If you want us to publish your piece, you have to make these changes." Walker knew what was at stake. She was silent for a moment, then gathered up her manuscript and stood to leave. "It's you who do not understand," she told them. "All I have to do in life is save my soul."

Alice Walker's response was more than an appropriate

refusal to the editors. It was a poetic statement of her determination to protect her being, the essence of who she was. It was, as well, a wonderful motto for a satisfying life, one worthy of mounting in large letters in places where we can't miss seeing it and being reminded on a daily basis:

All we have to do in life is save our souls.

If Walker had compromised her writing at that early point in her career to get published and make some much needed money, it might have set a pattern that would have detracted from the outspoken character of her work, a critical component in the great success she ultimately achieved. The message for me was that even — maybe especially — in a society where going along to get along is the unspoken rule of the game, standing your ground on matters that affect your sense of who you are can improve the chances of success while sustaining the values of an ethical life.

The examples of the young professor and Alice Walker are about moments of self-definition that set the standard for an ethical life. Sometimes, however, we are not in a position to take that sort of principled stand – at least in the moment – without it amounting to self-sabotage. Most law school courses grade students by one exam at the end, a final exam, from two to four hours in length. As you can imagine, the tension is great, particularly for first-year students being subjected to the process for the first time. The exam questions are highly complex and the time to answer each one must be carefully apportioned. A whole semester's work is at risk. Aware of the stakes, some professors throw in a question perhaps designed to separate the feeling from the unfeeling students, hoping to cull the latter into a Communion of the Insensate. Predictably, the question has an adverse affect. For example, a student told me that in her first-year contracts final exam, one question asked if, under contract law, a white aunt had the right to disinherit a black grandnephew because he was black. Ethically, the aunt's action was abominable, but arguing legally that she could not disinherit her grandnephew would be next to impossible. Because it is a will, the nephew has no contract, no expectation, no reliance – nor do most people as to someone else's will.

In all likelihood some white students and all the black students were shocked and hurt by the question. And yet there was no time to complain of the professor's lack of sensitivity, to say nothing of decency, in requiring the students to address an issue of blatant racial bias likely permitted under the common law. The students had to write an answer recognizing and defending the aunt's right, or fail. At the very least, students stunned by the question would lose valuable time while they got their emotions under control. For the black students, providing the answer the professor expected must have felt like systematically disowning themselves. In effect, answering the question correctly became a defeat for those students who felt the professor's intended slight.

When my students ask what they should do when a professor makes comments of this character in class, I tell them to start at the source and discuss the matter with the professor. If, as often happens, the teacher refuses to take it seriously ("Oh, when I said we went coon hunting down South, I meant raccoon, not a racial epithet. Don't be so sensitive!"), I urge the student to write the professor a letter spelling out her dissatisfaction. If this fails to gain an apology and a promise to be more careful, then she should take it to the dean. This is not easy advice to follow, because most students fear that the anonymous grading system is not really anonymous. Paranoid or not, I tell them that they need to take action that will get the matter off their backs and out of their hearts.

For members of subordinated groups and progressive thinkers of all backgrounds, resistance to insult and abuse is a powerful motivator precisely because it enables us to fulfill our longing to achieve our goals while letting us name the obstacles to those achievements. It enables us to resolve our ambivalence about success by giving us a reason to succeed that is embedded in a history of the social justice movements that have made success possible for us. Resistance-motivated success allows us to give priority to our beliefs over our desires. Such balance gives meaning to our work and our lives.

The road to success must at least seem smoother for those who keep silent in the face of insult or injustice. After all, despite racial barriers, a growing number of black people – not just the celebrities of sports and entertainment – are achieving success resembling current standards of status and income. For many, though, their achievement comes at a price that sometimes, in my view, is not worth paying. As they climb the ladder of success, they leave their values on the rungs amidst slights, insults, and outright injustice. They "arrive" well heeled and moderately respected by nearly everyone but themselves. Ellis Cose's 1993 book, *The Rage of a Privileged Class*, provides painful evidence of such unhappy compromises.

Cose interviewed dozens of highly successful black people who smiled their designer-fashion looks on the outside while seething inwardly from the racial slights from which their success did not protect them. The blacks Cose interviewed chose to protect their status by not protesting the discrimination that clouded their achievements. I've never worked in a corporate setting, but the many years I've spent working at large institutions enable me to imagine the difficulties. You have to simultaneously function on a high level and try not to upset those whose racial equilibrium is thrown off when they recognize that you are not incompetent, not mediocre, and don't fit the long-accepted notions about persons of color that serve as unrecognized but important components of their self-esteem. Even if we were to set aside for the moment considerations of ethical rectitude, we can see that the major unnamed fringe benefits of this dynamic are self-loathing and a corrosive resentment.

Does this mean that outsiders of all stripes – black, Latino, Asian, gay, lesbian . . . – should avoid corporate employment altogether? Hardly – there are challenges for even straight white men with conventional good looks, impeccable pedigrees, and family fortunes who are trying to retain their humanity in a corporate environment. If we sought to steer clear of situations that challenged us ethically we would make our lives extremely narrow – and not necessarily ethical. Let us not assume that speaking out in defense of ourselves, our group, or what we believe in will have the worst possible consequences. In fact, let us assume that not speaking out is the very thing that may lead to the outcome we consider the least desirable of all.

Most protests that come to public attention are mounted by groups rather than individuals. There can be strength in numbers, but even great numbers cannot ensure the safety of those engaged in protest against a powerful and entrenched authority: There are risks one takes simply by being a member of a group. Intimidation, threats, and actual physical violence are unethical and often illegal, particularly when brought to bear against an individual or group lacking the means to respond or defend itself effectively. Those who oppose abortion on religious grounds are entitled to exercise their First Amendment rights to protest such procedures, but courts have properly enjoined harassment tactics at clinics or the homes of physicians that include in-the-face yelling, often while brandishing bottled fetuses, blocking entrances, and other tactics intended less to convince than to intimidate and terrorize those wishing to avail themselves of their constitutional rights.

The student sit-ins of the early 1960s at soda fountains, restaurants, and other racially segregated public facilities are a paradigmatic illustration of ethical protests. To oppose hateful policies, the protesting students placed their bodies in the seats within the facilities where but for their race they would have been served. In effect, they risked arrest and bodily harm in order to raise for public debate and, they hoped, eventual resolution, the issue of segregation – still legal in privately owned facilities open to the public. That, as we know, is what happened. Their protests did honor to themselves and gave store owners reason to reconsider the continued value of racial polices that had become economic liabilities.

I don't want to minimize the financial risks and the physical and emotional costs involved in the risk of being ethical. These risks are enormous when individuals charge a major corporation with any form of actionable discrimination. Bari-Ellen Roberts was a vice president at one of the world's largest and most prestigious banks when Texaco, the country's fourth largest oil company, recruited her with promises of professional challenge and advancement. What she found there was a persistent pattern of racial discrimination against her and fourteen hundred other African American employees. In her book, *Roberts vs. Texaco*, she sets forth her experiences and the long and complex litigation in which she was the lead plaintiff.[7]

Despite herculean efforts by her lawyers, Texaco managed to stall the litigation for years and would likely have prevailed had not a disgruntled white executive, forced into retirement, come forth with taped recordings of meetings where high-level Texaco executives conspired to destroy documents sought by the plaintiffs. Adding insult to injury, the executives were recorded calling black employees black jelly beans and other racial epithets. Under a barrage of bad publicity and falling stock prices, Texaco settled the case for $176 million and agreed to an outside task force to review hiring and promotional polices intended to eradicate the corporate culture of bigotry that made the law suit necessary.[8]

Initially the prospects of a legal victory were no better for a group of black employees who filed an employment discrimination lawsuit against the mammoth Coca-Cola Company. They signed on to the case because they were unwilling to continue to silently acquiesce when they were routinely passed over for promotions, receiving less pay than the white subordinates they trained or supervised, and averaging $26,000 a year less in salary than white employees. After years of litigation and negotiation, they gained a settlement worth $192.5 million, as well as getting the company to approve a seven-member task force that has substantial authority to set hiring and promotional policies.[9] The plaintiffs' determination, faith, and courage led to vindication and monetary damages for all other black employees at Texaco and Coca-Cola. Their real triumph, though, was in the decision the plaintiffs made to mount challenges against powerful conglomerates, knowing that their chances of prevailing were very small.

Inspiring words, but those contemplating filing employment discrimination suits in today's unsympathetic legal climate must consider the obstacles. Unemployment, harassment, strikebreakers, and blacklisting, to name a few, are among the retaliatory measures used when just claims threaten the profit margins of large corporations. However, despite the conservative political climate – especially because of that climate – it is crucial that we challenge unjust work practices and health threats as a group. It may sound naïvely idealistic, but it is only our ability to take action as a group that provides real checks and balance in a democratic society. Group struggle is hard, sometimes the hardest of risks, because at any point the urge to leave the struggle to others can so easily justify our not continuing. But it is also the most honorable, the most clearly selfless of all the risks because its immediate effect on others is so palpable.

I certainly don't want to convey the sense that leaving jobs or challenging unjust practices in them is easy. Doing so is traumatic as well as cathartic. When my protests led to resignations, I took with me my professional status and sufficient experience, to say nothing of some savings in the bank, all of which made it feasible to move on when job situations became dicey. But not everyone has transferable job skills, flexibility, and a very supportive life partner whose income would help them maintain an even financial keel. I was not wealthy, but I realized that not everyone who might have joined me in my job protests had even my modest financial stability. And that is why perhaps the greatest benefit of pulling oneself out of poverty and avoiding the consumer addiction that leads to oppressive debt is the freedom that financial independence provides. I learned the lesson of the incalculable value of financial independence from my mother.

Having said this, I don't think the availability of money to pay the bills is the essential prerequisite to those who challenge authority. That prerequisite is the burning sense that a wrong must be addressed and an abiding faith that while it may involve risk, things will work out in the long run. This is something I saw demonstrated in my family for as far back as I can remember.

My mother was an early model for my determination to challenge rather than go along with actions I believe are wrong. My family lived in the Hill, a mainly black area of Pittsburgh, Pennsylvania. One day when I was six or seven years old, my mother, Ada Childress Bell, took my brother Charles and me with her to the rent office. My mother, standing in front of the barred teller's window, took cash from her purse and waved it in front of the clerk. That is all I really remember, but I learned later that she told him: "This is the rent money. I have it – and you will get it when you fix the back steps so that my children won't fall and hurt themselves." Then, we left the office.

It was not until many years later that I recognized my mother's strength. She was willing to face eviction to gain a safe home for her family, the right to which was not then recognized by the law and would not be for decades. It was in the midst of the Great Depression and in those economically dreary times my father worked as a laborer whenever he could find a job. We had no savings, and had the landlord evicted us for nonpayment of rent, we really had no place to go.

"What happened?" I asked.

My mother, even many years later, beamed. "They fixed the steps," she said proudly. "And," she added, "they fixed all the steps along the row of houses where we lived."

Even more years later, I asked her, "Did your neighbors know what you did?"

"Not from me, they didn't," she replied, and then noting my surprise, answered the question I would have asked. "Many of those people were friends. I didn't want them to feel beholden to me for something I did for my family, something," she added, "I did for myself."

Her story gave me a keen insight into the subtleties of confronting those in authority. What I have learned from her, from many others, and from my experience, I can encompass in three points.

First, while I recognize the risks, there is always the possibility that a polite but firm statement will lead to a change of policy or put the implementers on notice that their actions are unacceptable to at least some of the group members.

Second, even when the complaint or protest is rejected out of hand, confronting those in authority nurtures your sense of dignity and can have strange and unpredictable ways of enhancing rather than diminishing chances for a satisfying job with rewarding work.

Third, while these first two points are praiseworthy, neither offers sufficient motivation for most of us to do the right thing that is usually the hard thing — to take unpopular stands, to risk well-being, income, and in some situations, even our lives. The matter which occasions a response, a protest, is usually one that has troubled us a great deal, upset our insides, monopolized our thoughts. Miraculously, when I stand up and speak out, expressing an unpopular view strongly, fully aware that it is neither welcomed nor likely to be heeded by those in authority, I experience a unique sense of peace. It is that peace that I wish for my students and children more than anything else. I know more powerfully than ever that inner peace is worth more than succumbing to apathy, and more than any material gain. To risk ethically is a difficult blessing, but whatever the outcome, to risk ethically is also to live.

CHAPTER THREE

EVOLVING FAITH

Now, faith is the substance of things hoped for,
the evidence of things not seen.
The Epistle of Paul to the Hebrews, 11:1

Do not tell lies and do not do what you hate.
The Gospel of Thomas from the Gnostics

G RACE ELLEN, a law student only a few months away
from graduation, stopped by my office for a visit.
Impressive, personable, very bright and quite thoughtful,
Grace Ellen turned her back on lucrative law firm offers in
favor of a career in legal service to the disadvantaged. She
believed deeply in the mission of the nonprofit organization
for which she was currently working, but found herself
frustrated by the external barriers thwarting their programs
and internal politics that so easily distracted the staff.

Hearing the weariness in her voice, I tried to reassure her.
"Working for the public interest, you are always going to
be, as one gospel song puts it, 'climbing up the rough side of
the mountain.' It's a tough task, Grace Ellen. You need as

much help from others and perseverance from within as you can muster."

Dismayed, she asked me how I had remained committed to social reform efforts when, as she put it, "The frustrations are many and endless, while the satisfactions are few and fleeting."

"I have relied on my faith. Particularly in hard times, my Christian faith provides reassurance that is unseen but no less real. It never fails to give me the fortitude I need when opposing injustice despite the almost certain failure of my action to persuade those in authority to alter their plans or policies. For me it is my most powerful resource."

Grace Ellen seemed taken aback by my response. "Well," she said, choosing her words with great care, "I guess I'm a Christian, but I just don't believe in the things a Christian is supposed to believe in – the virgin birth, the miracles, the resurrection. I even have trouble with imagining God as a supernatural being who controls all that happens in the world, punishing evil and rewarding good. I want to believe, but I can't fake it for purposes of fire insurance."

Grace Ellen's words touched me deeply. I'd like to report that I reached into a bag of wisdom and pulled out the answers she was looking for. I did tell her what she likely already knew, namely that there are many spiritual paths, not to mention faiths not centered on religion of any kind. I acknowledged that many ethical people want nothing to do with organized religion, but they view life as a gift with an obligation to uplift the lives of those around them. These people, paradoxically, may be closer to living the life that Jesus urged than many who adhere to the doctrines of one of the Christian denominations. Just as there are those who are religious but have little faith, there are those who claim no religion and yet have concepts of living that define real faith.

Telling Grace Ellen this may have been helpful, but it was far from the explanation she was seeking as to the role of faith in my life. I have no desire to proselytize others. I want, though, to convey my recognition that it is faith that provides me the emotional fuel, the kinetic connection to the others elements of my character. By exploring my own evolving understanding of how my faith serves as the foundation of my effort to live an ethical life, I want to explain to Grace Ellen and to others my reliance on what theologian Paul Tillich calls "a faith beyond the unbelievable." From my upbringing in a church blessed with music, I experienced a reawakening of my faith in the civil rights movement.

For much of my life, I did not much worry about defining my faith, believing was enough. I was brought up in the church, but knew little about theology or denominational policies. My parents had me baptized at an early age in a large African-Methodist-Episcopal (AME) church in Pittsburgh. Later, I joined a black Presbyterian church where I sang in the choir during my high school and, as I recall, most of my college years. My mother hoped I would become a preacher, but she never pushed her hopes and I felt then that one needed to be called in some fashion similar to Paul's encounter with God on the road to Damascus.

My religious faith is closely tied to music, particularly spirituals and gospel hymns. As a young child, sent across the street to the store on a Sunday morning, I would not miss a beat of the radio broadcast of the Negro choir Wings Over Jordan. I could hear their music through the open windows of our neighbors in those pre-air-conditioner days. Many years later, I obtained a few long-play recordings of the Wings Over Jordan choir. Hearing their a cappella renderings of the old spirituals "Take Me to the Water," "A Deep River," "I Will Trust in the Lord" magically transports me back some sixty years when even as a child I was impressed with both the beauty and the fervor of their singing. I never heard Marian Anderson in concert, but listening to her recordings of spirituals, I hear not simply a marvelous voice, but a reverence for the music that offers the listener a direct line to the spirit of God.

The spirituals of course were composed by my forebears who survived hundreds of years of a slavery that denied them both their freedom and their personhood. To pacify them, their masters read them carefully selected biblical Scriptures. Somehow, beyond the literal words they heard, they sensed Jesus' message of salvation and found the spirit that fortified them in their lifelong ordeal. The slave singers recognized and identified with the despair and hopelessness of the Old Testament Israelites. By interweaving melody and lyric in songs of faith – the spirituals – they were able to transcend the awful oppression that defined their lives. The music was their legacy, quite literally a theology in song.

The message in the spirituals is universal. A few years ago, Jessye Norman sang a series of three concerts at Carnegie Hall devoted to the greatest songs in the classical repertoire, including those written by Strauss, Brahms, Schubert. Each section was warmly received by the large and mainly white audience. When, though, as an encore at one of the concerts, Ms Norman sang the spiritual "He's Got the Whole World in His Hands," the audience leapt to its feet, erupting in a frenzy of emotionally laden shouts and applause. Her artistry and this music had transformed this classical audience into a church enthused with the spirit.

For much of my life, I have been swept along, lifted up really, by the sense that I was part of a religious tradition that earned salvation by doing good works, trying to live a good life. My belief in Christ did not limit me to Christian doctrine. On the contrary, while I did not fully appreciate it at the time, what most attracted me to the teachings of Christ was his courage and his vision of radical inclusiveness. The teachings of Jesus were revelatory and revolutionary. Christianity should embrace, not exclude.

I was far from alone in experiencing a nurturing of that faith during the civil rights movement's mighty effort to end the oppression of racial segregation. The movement's commitment to nonviolent protest, with its tactical as well as moral motivations, enraged and frustrated those in power in ways not unlike the early Christians when they courageously stood up to the awesome power of Rome when doing so meant almost certain death.

Civil rights activists were often in violent situations that could and sometimes did result in arrest, serious injuries, and sometimes death. Dr Martin Luther King, Jr, saw himself as a modern-day Christian prepared for martyrdom. In his 1963 Letter from a Birmingham Jail, one of the great theological papers of the twentieth century, King responded to a group of ministers who publicly criticized his leadership of the marches that led to violent reactions by the police and some whites. Dr King reminded the clergymen of the origins of the Christian church when the emphasis was on the spirit and not church politics. "There was a time," said King, "when the church was not very powerful, in the time when the early Christians rejoiced at being deemed worthy to suffer for what they believed." Utilizing his inimitable way with language, King wrote:

In those days the church was not merely a thermometer that recorded the ideas and principles of popular opinion; it was a thermostat that transformed the mores of society. Whenever the early Christians entered a town, the people in power became disturbed and immediately sought to convict the Christians for being "disturbers of the peace" and "outside agitators," but the Christians pressed on in the conviction that they were "a colony of heaven," called to obey God rather than man. Small in number, they were big in commitment.[10]

In his letter, King wondered when this all changed. When did power built on wealth and political influence become the basis to intimidate rather than illuminate a congregation with descriptions of God's power? Whatever the causes, King said, too often the Christian church has kept Christ in its name, but not in its heart. The sign of the cross, he conceded, can raise huge edifices to the church, but too often has lost its power to transform human souls to Christ.

While he hoped and prayed for victory in his work for racial and economic justice, King recognized a value beyond achievement of his goals. In one essay, "Testament of Hope,"[11] published after his death, Dr King speaks of his setbacks, the time he spent in jails, his frustrations and sorrows, and the dangerous character of his adversaries; he knew those adversaries expected him to harden into a grim and desperate man. But he writes: "They fail, however, to perceive the sense of affirmation generated by the challenge of embracing struggle and surmounting obstacles."

His words echoed the sentiment of one of his inspirations, Mahatma Gandhi, the great Hindu leader, whose nonviolent campaign wrested India from British colonialism. In a letter to a friend, Gandhi declared: "Speak the truth, without fear and without exception, and see everyone whose work is related to your purpose. You are in God's work, so you need not fear men's scorn. If they listen to your requests and accept them, you will be satisfied. If they reject them, then you must make their rejection your strength."[12]

Like Jesus before him, Dr King communicated by his words and in his actions a deeper message of commitment to courageous struggle whatever the circumstances, the odds, or the outcome. A part of that struggle was the need to speak the truth as he viewed it even when that truth alienated rather than unified, upset minds rather than calmed hearts, and subjected the speaker to general censure rather than acclaim. In this, I believe Dr King represented the essence, the true spirit of Christianity.

Grace Ellen is far from alone in finding that church doctrine and rules of conduct are more confusing and off-putting than enlightening and uplifting. Intended to strengthen faith, church canons and creeds actually serve to maintain church dominance, all too often at the expense of strengthening the faith of the faithful. The possible origin of the disparity in Christian creeds and faith were captured for me by Nikos Kazantzakis's novel *The Last Temptation of Christ*. In a scene following the Last Supper, Jesus tells his disciples that he must die as foretold by the prophets. They weep and wail, urging him not to leave, or to take them with him. One of them, though, Jacob, quickly reconciles himself to Jesus' death and promises that the disciples will ensure that his words shall not perish.

"We'll establish them firmly in new Holy Scriptures, we'll make laws, build our own synagogues and select our own high priests, Scribes and Pharisees."

Jesus is horrified. "You crucify the spirit, Jacob," he shouted. "No, no, I don't want that!"

Jacob tries to reassure him. "This is the only way we can prevent the spirit from turning into air and escaping."

"But it won't be free any more; it won't be spirit!"

"That doesn't matter," Jacob responds. "It will look like spirit. For our work, Rabbi, that's sufficient."[13]

The "sufficiency" that looks like spirit has served as the structure that the Christian church has used for its survival and growth as an institution. All too often, though, as Kazantzakis observed, the structure has replaced the spirit it was supposed to support and enhance. Form and ritual have taken on such importance that some can feel comfortable breaking every ethical rule in the book during the week because, on Sunday, they attend church and assume their sins are forgiven.

Emphasis on structural beliefs as tests of faith rather than the development of spiritual power has served to rationalize the necessity of unquestioned adherence to church doctrines drawn from the Bible's often contradictory admonitions. Treating the Bible as infallible requires ignoring what we know of modern science, technology, knowledge beyond anything those living in the first century could possibly have imagined. The application of literal interpretations to issues involving race, women's rights, anti-Semitism, abortion, and homosexuality, among other matters, has led to results that are unjust, unfair, and, to my lay mind, far from Christian. The claim, for example, that homosexuality must be deemed an abomination because Leviticus 18:22 and other verses are so interpreted, would also authorize the purchase of slaves as long as they are "of the heathen that are round about you (Leviticus 25:44). Exodus 35:2 clearly authorizes putting to death anyone who works on the Sabbath, a holy day. And Genesis 39:9–10 suggests that even birth control may be a capital offense.

These admonitions and many like them are not followed, but neither adverse publicity nor the contrary wishes of much of their memberships have moved many Christian churches to reconsider their barring of women from the clergy by either official mandate or long tradition. The usual justification is that Jesus did not choose any women to be his disciples. Such literalness ignores the social order in the first century in which a woman member of a disciple band of an itinerant rabbi was inconceivable.[14]

Grace Ellen and likely a great many others are over-whelmed by the contradictions between what they are told they must believe in church and what they experience in the world. With so much attention to scriptural interpretation, there is little thought given to the fact that Jesus preached a radical inclusiveness that people of his day could no more tolerate than most can in our time. It was the preaching of that inclusiveness, Rev. James Hightower maintains, that got Jesus nailed to the cross. Modern Christian churches tend to forgo the revolutionary essence of Jesus' message, preaching instead that Jesus died for our sins and thus we must honor his sacrifice by our commitment to him through the church. By giving priority to the rituals of worship, we neglect what Rev. Peter Gomes calls "the sublime logic of his teaching [and] the undaunted example of his life."[15]

Of course, we should not be so contemptuous of those who take the Christian myth *literally*, that we fail to take it *seriously*. By particularizing the Bible, the literalists trivialize the depth of its meaning and the universality of its message. Faith, taken seriously, while challenged by this new knowledge, has the potential to fortify rather than destroy a belief that is not rigid, that is evolving with the experiences of life and learning. This is Reinhold Niebuhr's view, one that is shared by many biblical scholars. They do not deny that a literal belief in the biblical stories was important in the development of the early church. Many find not literal truth but spiritual meaning in even the most fantastic elements in the Christian narrative, including the reports of Jesus healing the sick and raising the dead.

Peter Laarman, minister of New York City's famous Judson Church, explains that "these biblical narratives can be history-*like* without needing to be historical." The Gospel stories' purpose, Laarman maintains, is "to *narrate the identity of Jesus by showing us the kind of person Jesus was*. The test of their truth is not whether the incidents they describe took place, but whether they truthfully narrate the identity of Jesus to us."[16] The belief that this suffering servant was raised to glorious life, whether or not literally true, Laarman suggests, can make sense of our lives and provide an adequate symbol of life-giving hope.

Contemporary theologians have pieced together what little is known about Jesus of Nazareth. His was a quite short résumé. Jesus was born in Judea, a subject of Rome under Caesar Augustus. He lived only about three decades, with most of his teaching – deemed subversive and dangerous by the authorities – occurring during the last few years of his life. As a Jew, Jesus lived under the harsh occupation of Rome as administered by Jewish overseers whose positions depended on their ability to keep the peace. As Dr Howard Thurman put it, if a Roman soldier pushed Jesus into a ditch, he could not appeal to Caesar. As far as the law was concerned, Jesus was simply another Jew in a ditch. In all his years, there was not a moment in which he was free.[17] Under Roman rule, anyone who challenged the existing powers was identified, arrested, and summarily executed. Aware of the danger, the Jewish population in the area was nevertheless far from content in their conquered state. They awaited the coming of a Messiah, a man of war who would lead a revolt and overthrow the Romans. And there were several uprisings, all of them put down thoroughly and brutally by the Roman soldiers.

Jesus' teaching that because God loved humanity, Christians, in order to please God, had to love one another as well as those beyond the family and the group, was a major departure from religion as generally known. The idea that God loves those who love him was entirely new in a pagan world where a host of gods and goddesses cared little for one another and even less for humans. Jesus was only one of several individuals who led small groups that the rulers viewed as dangers to the peace. There was no distinction between religious and political rule. When Jesus spoke of the kingdom of heaven as the ultimate power rather than the majesty of Rome, he threatened those who held both religious and political power. When great numbers of people began to follow him and heed his teachings, his execution was a virtual certainty. Indeed, the one fact about Jesus about which there is no dispute is that he was condemned by order of the Roman prefect, Pontius Pilate, and in A.D. 30 was crucified, the form of execution the Romans used for political prisoners.

Modern scholars have traced how the resurrection and ascension legends grew over time, noting their similarity to phenomena in the Old Testament and from other religions. In every way they could imagine, these early Christian writers were determined to convey what an important life Jesus led. Over time, though, the legends created to bolster a faith based on the revolutionary in Jesus' teachings evolved into rules of behavior and belief. It is precisely what, in Kazantzakis's novel, Jesus feared would happen.

As with so much in life, it is easier for me to say what God is not than to explain to others – and to myself – what God is. As my faith evolves, I feel quite comfortable agreeing with Rev. Peter Laarman that I can still take part in the rituals of Christmas and Easter. The birth and death of Jesus remain important concepts worthy of celebration even if the details are not what so many continue to believe are literally true. I can continue to gain comfort and insight from reading the Bible, and continue to say grace before meals and lower my head in prayer in church. In all these endeavors, I know that God is there, even if not in the form I had long imagined.

As my faith evolves, I find value in the Gnostics, an early Christian sect who accepted the word but interpreted it differently. Elaine Pagels, in her fine and accessible book *The Gnostic Gospels* (from the Greek, reflective knowledge, insight), reports that the Gnostics' works describe many of the people and events found in the New Testament, but do so from a startlingly different perspective on early Christianity.[18] Some of their texts, discovered only in the last half-century, deny the resurrection of Jesus, believing his divinity proven by his teachings. Pagels examines and compares the Gnostic views with those adopted by what became the orthodox (literally, "straight-thinking") Christian church. The orthodox church drove the Gnostics to the periphery of the Christian world, dismissing their views as preposterous.

The essence of the Gnostic teachings was that the presence of the divine is within each human and that the road to salvation is through self-knowledge. Some Gnostic groups believed in God as both father and mother. They held that women and men were spiritual equals, an equality long denied by the orthodox church. The Gnostic, then, was one who sought to understand everything possible about one's self. To know self at the deepest level, they believed, is to know God. As Monoimus, one of its ancient teachers, urged:

Abandon the search for God and the creation and other matters of a similar sort. Look for him by taking yourself at the starting point. Learn who it is within you who makes everything his own and says, "My God, my mind, my thought, my soul, my body." Learn the sources of sorrow, joy, love, hate . . . if you carefully investigate these matters you will find him *in yourself.*[19]

I find it amazing that this early Gnostic Christian was able to escape from the limitations of a time when it was reasonable to believe that the earth was flat, that heaven was just beyond the clouds, and hell was somewhere below the earth. Belief in a theistic God, that is, a supernatural ruler of the universe, was universal among the Jews and, in different form, among the early Christians. Philosophers tell us that belief in such a being relieved the anxiety that humans felt with their selfhood and the uncertain limits of life. A theistic God offered stability and the sense that someone all-powerful was in charge. Belief in this theistic God is now undermined by what science and technology have taught us about the world, knowledge that has created a new anxiety and uncertainty and led many to take refuge in fundamentalism. Somehow, Monoimus and surely others were able to leap across centuries of learning to a perception of God that is similar to what some contemporary theologians envision.

In our time, Bishop John Shelby Spong, for many years the Episcopal bishop in Newark, New Jersey, has been among the theologians who have pioneered in pushing the boundaries of traditional Christian belief. In his writings, he has tried to explain the need in the early Christian church for belief that Jesus was the intended product of a theistic God who arranged for his virgin birth and his resurrection. He advocates, I think in terms quite like Monoimus, that we now must seek a new vision of the holy that is beyond theism but within the reality for which the word God was created.

Acknowledging that much of what I have learned and believed about Jesus is myth simply opens the door to understanding what it was about Jesus and his life that led those who knew of him to see the need to create the myths in the first place.

Likely because of their reliance on self-knowledge as the knowledge of God rather than structure and doctrine, the

Gnostics, as Nikos Kazantzakis's Jacob predicted, did not have the staying power and the organizational potential of the approach that became orthodox Christianity. There are, though, attractive elements in their reliance on the individual to obtain knowledge of God and salvation, not through any particular regime, but through constant self-examination and self-improvement. An example of the self-discovery that appears key in many of the writings is found in the Gospel of Thomas, perhaps the most cited of the Gnostic Gospels, and one that is limited to the teachings of Jesus without any description of his life. Thomas writes:

> His disciples questioned him and said to him, "Do you want us to fast? How shall we pray? Shall we give alms? What diet shall we observe?"
>
> Jesus replied: "Do not tell lies, and do not do what you hate . . ."[20]

Elaine Pagels points out that his ironic answer turns the disciples' questions back to them. Each person must judge when one is lying or doing what one hates. It is not constraining. It is liberating. Imagine the great wisdom in both trying to follow these simple admonitions and the benefit of such adherence to others and to one's self. For me, the advice is revelatory regarding life and about a Jesus that I can understand. It is similar to much of the teachings of Jesus contained in the Gospels. It is also universal.

The message: "Do not tell lies, and do not do what you hate" refutes the widespread belief that living a life of faith requires living a life of moral, spiritual, and religious perfection. Its urging is likely one of the reasons so many people flee from organized religion. Instead, living a faithful life means as the slave singer urged: "Keep your hand on the plow. Hold on." Hold on during periods of life when our confidence in ourselves and our faith is the weakest. It is faith in our fate and foresight about our future that provides us with the endurance, dexterity, and flexibility required to live a life of meaning and worth.

There is an unresolved and perhaps an unresolvable dilemma here. For Nikos Kazantzakis's portrayal of Jesus and Jacob are both correct. Without structure, leadership, rules, and required practices, church leaders feared there would not be the organization needed to survive and grow. That protective structure, though, has tended to stifle the Christian spirit and replace it with doctrines regarding who can join the church, what they must do, how they must live. Dos and don'ts to be obeyed rather than questions to be asked and answered on a daily basis. For Jacob, all of these rules and procedures were a necessary sacrifice: "It will look like spirit," he assures Jesus. "For our work, Rabbi, that's sufficient." For many Christians, though, the struggle to accept the literal belief in a superhuman God on high, and to adhere to rules that no longer make sense in the modern world, obscures the revelatory wonders of the life that Jesus lived and the conditions under which he died. In such instances, simply "looking like spirit" misses the essence of the Christian message.

The dilemma of the Christian church then is quite like the dilemma with which we as individuals must contend as we try to both succeed and hold on to our integrity. The gravitational pulls of our "free enterprise" society urge acceptance of the social system as it is. It counsels us to compete and win by any available means. As needed, we can pretend we are ethical and humane. Our posturing will look like spirit and it will appear sufficient. The challenge for those with ethical ambition is to transform the symbolically sufficient into the substantively real.

CHAPTER FOUR

ADVANCING
RELATIONSHIPS

Our intimate relationships with family, friends,
and life partners are the foundation
of an ethical life.

I BEGAN THINKING ABOUT this chapter almost as soon
as I formed the idea for this book. When I mentioned this
to an old friend, he gave me a perplexed look. "But if you're
writing about ethical ambition and ethical success, won't
every chapter be about relationships?" I smiled and nodded.
He had a point. However self-sufficient we may fancy
ourselves, we exist only *in relation* – to our friends, family,
and life partners; to those we teach and mentor; to our co-
workers, neighbors, strangers; and even (as I discussed in the
previous chapter) to forces we cannot fully conceive of, let
alone define. In many ways, we *are* our relationships. But
because the ubiquity and transcendent importance of our
connections with others is precisely the thing that often
renders them invisible to us, I decided to devote an entire
chapter to the subject.

When I'm asked for my thoughts about relationships – and for a law professor I'm asked surprisingly often – those thoughts tend first to marriage. This is not because I believe that marriage is the only kind of relationship worth contemplating. I account for my tendency to think of marriage first as simply evidence of what has been the most important relationship to me. Even then I cannot claim expertise so much as I can experience – I have been married more than half of my long life and my experience has turned me into an advocate. In this chapter I will explore the connection between marriage and ethical living, and venture from there to share a few thoughts about other kinds of relationships: those we have with family, friends, co-workers, and – as a teacher for over thirty years – students.

There is an old saying: "How fortunate is the person who has never loved and lost. How fortunate, and how sad." I have felt those words to be true for more years than I can count, and more deeply the longer I have lived. When I think on them, it is not with an understanding of "love" as romance, or as love affair, but as marriage. As one minister put it, "the person we marry is a stranger about whom we have a magnificent hunch."[21] There are risks, but the potential value, particularly for the ethically committed, is great.

Whether married or single, all ethical people strive to choose "right" over "easy" when confronted by situations that force them to choose one or the other. However, from my own experience, which has been affirmed by the experience of others, I have learned that marriage can be an invaluable support for those determined to stand up to and overcome the many challenges associated with leading an ethical life.

Perhaps I should put marriage in quotation marks, because to me it denotes not only those couples' relationships that are formalized by church and state, but those—and particularly those—that people think of as "committed relationships," regardless of the genders of those in the union, and whether or not that union is sanctioned by the larger society. I believe our own understanding of what constitutes marriage is of greater importance than how it may be defined by our institutions. That the laws of most countries recognize only unions between a man and a woman is testimony to what a slow and lumbering creature the law can be, and not to any ultimate validity of those laws. Let us remember that laws forbidding marriage between people of different races were still on the books in the United States until the Supreme Court declared them unconstitutional in 1967. If, as I so fervently believe, marriage can keep you in touch with your past, your emotional self, and your humanity, the notion that this should be any less true for gay or lesbian couples than it is for heterosexuals is absurd.

The challenges of marriage are many, but the rewards are

great. In forcing you to connect with your humanness, marriage can give you an identity not determined by the sometimes inhumane demands of the world outside the hearth. And here is where I rely on my experience: A major component in the success of many people has been the woman or man to whom they were married. I could say "husband" or "wife," but a far more accurate label is "life partner." In these marriages, both people are *full* partners in the relationship, their views valued and their advice followed (often, if not always).

One of my models of a workable partnership is the fifty-year marriage between eminent historian John Hope Franklin and his wife, Aurelia. As they wrote in *For Better, for Worse*, a booklet they published on their golden anniversary,

We early learned to respect each other's intellectual and professional interests . . . We had a practice of discussing our work with each other. We felt that each could offer suggestions or advice to the other as well as lend moral support . . . We have always felt that anything as important as one's professional activities must be shared in order for a couple to have a full appreciation of each other's work and activities . . . Both of us believe that a relationship can be shattered if one violates the rights, dignity, or privacy of the other. We also believe that a healthy relationship rests on absolute trust on both sides.

Consequently, we enjoy an independence not sullied by suspicion. We share the view that mutual respect is as essential in a marriage as it is in other relationships.[22]

It is hard to imagine a more effective recipe for a long and successful marriage. The Franklins were able to achieve a natural and healthy equality between partners where both did what they could without regard to who earned what, who held what degrees, and whose job or career was moving ahead faster. The fortuity of those facts never inspired resentment or recrimination.

This did not happen by magic, or because John Hope and Aurelia were saints. It happened because they saw themselves as members of a team: The good of one was the good of the other; harm or hurt to one was harm or hurt to the other. The basis of the relationship was an empathy enacted through respect. In short, the partnership enhances the couple's humanity by challenging each person to become more sensitive to and better able to rely on, respect, and cherish the other.

A marriage of sharing in career as well as in personal matters is not a phenomenon limited to the professional class. Following a lecture at a rather remote college, I was driven to the airport by a driver who turned out to be the owner of the limousine service. It was an early morning trip and his wife accompanied him. We somehow began talking about marriage, and he told me that he could not have built his successful business without his wife. She worked with him at every point, exercising what he called a "sixth sense" about business that enabled him to make several profitable decisions. She then told me about how she helped him *avoid* some decisions that would have been disastrous. I was gratified to hear their story of how marriage, with all its problems and challenges, offered them a life that was both fulfilling and successful. And I told them that my experience had been much like theirs.

During every day of our thirty years together, my late wife, Jewel Hairston Bell, played a crucial part in my ongoing education, in molding the person I am. She was mother of our three sons, confidant, advisor, and best friend. I had known her since childhood – we both came from working-class families in Pittsburgh and had been classmates in junior and senior high – but it wasn't until we met again nine years later that I began to see her in a different light. We had, unbeknown to each other, both moved to Washington, D.C. Learning that I was there, she called and invited me to attend service with her at a newly formed Church of the Redeemer.

The church was started by a young minister, Rev. Jefferson Rogers, whom we both admired. Rogers was important in my life for two reasons. First, he had resigned as pastor from a prestigious black church because he found the congregation hopelessly bourgeois, and more interested in status than doing the Lord's work. I was impressed that, far from suffering as a result of his action, Rogers was enthused with his work in starting a new church.

Second, Jewel and I spent many happy hours in the Rogerses' home with his wife, Mary Grace, and their three young children. During those visits, I began to see that marriage could support rather than burden my ambitions if I found the right person. And as I watched Jeff Rogers, one of the best-read persons I know, and Jewel argue for hours over any of a variety of subjects, it seemed clear that Jewel was that person.

Listening as she more than held her own in those debates, I began remembering the qualities I had so appreciated in our school days.

She was still smart, of course, but also articulate and self-assured in a way that I did not remember as a teenager. Even more impressive was how personable she was, and our common backgrounds provided a basis for easy comfort and sharing. Then there was something else: Jewel had an insight into people that bordered on the supernatural, giving her an uncanny power of understanding people's thoughts and feelings with an acuity that left me breathless. Her professional training had only served to heighten these skills.

The next summer she was program director at the Urban League–sponsored James Weldon Johnson Summer Camp for black children, a position I had held a few years earlier, and where we had *both* been counselors years before. I visited her at the camp and one evening, under the stars, I asked her to marry me. To my everlasting good fortune, she said yes, and we were married not long afterward.

I was twenty-nine, and Jewel was twenty-eight. I had just joined the staff of the NAACP Legal Defense Fund. She had her own career as a psychiatric social worker, and continued to pursue it with energy and success, but she still managed to be a bulwark of support during the years when I had to spend weeks at a time away from home. First it was handling civil rights cases in the Deep South, and then travel for the Department of Health, Education and Welfare. I left my family in Washington for three months when I accepted the position heading a new poverty law center at the University of Southern California Law School. By then we had three sons, and Jewel had left social work to be a full-time mom, providing stability to a home from which I was often absent.

I get credit for becoming the first tenured black professor at the Harvard Law School, but I could never have survived the very real pressures of being that kind of pioneer without Jewel. I knew that overcoming the assumptions of racial inadequacy would not be easy, but I soon saw that another challenge would be bridging the class gap between the white faculty members and myself. They had all gone to prestigious colleges where they'd done extremely well, and then on to top-line law schools where they won academic honors and edited their schools' law journals. After law school, most had clerked at the Supreme Court and, perhaps after a few years at major law firms, joined the faculty at Harvard, which they considered the nation's best law school.

If that series of achievements constituted the checklist of criteria for being a professor at Harvard Law School, I would have had to check the box marked "none of the above." I had handled civil rights cases throughout the South, but with few exceptions major law schools do not honor litigators; indeed, those with substantial litigation experience are looked upon with suspicion. After all, it is felt, those with real intellectual potential would not waste their time in what is deemed vocational labor. I believed in what I had done, and I knew my achievements were worthwhile, but in my first years at Harvard the differences in our backgrounds and legal experiences sometimes brought on feelings of inadequacy. I remember listening quietly and with some discomfort to lunchroom conversations where faculty members boasted about the opinions they had written for the Supreme Court justices under whom they had served.

To make matters worse, there was no one who shared my ideas about pedagogy. I could imagine no positive value in teaching my classes on the *Paper Chase* model, but I could find few people who wanted to discuss alternatives. As a result, I had to pioneer an approach in the classroom and in my writing that made sense to me. This took years of hard work for me, *and* for Jewel, who was my supportive editor. Without her understanding and constant encouragement, I simply would not have made it. Whenever it appeared that the pressures were getting to me, Jewel would reassure me that, though different, I deserved to be there. She reminded me that none of my elite colleagues had accomplished what I had as a civil rights lawyer and administrator. I slowly overcame my fears based on difference, and formulated a style of teaching and writing that featured that difference.

My Harvard agreement called for me to serve for two years, after which the faculty would vote on whether or not they would offer me tenure. As the time for the tenure review approached, a member of the Appointments Committee told me that while my civil rights course was going well, the first-year criminal law course I had volunteered to teach needed more work, and suggested that I request a postponement of the review for a year. When I told Jewel she was furious. "Tell them no! You've worked hard for two years and kept your part of the bargain. Now they have to decide what to do, after which we will decide what to do. Remember, dear," she added firmly, "Harvard needs us. We do not need Harvard." I agreed with her, and turned down the suggestion of the "extra" year. A few weeks later, the tenured faculty voted and my tenure was approved.

Even during her years-long battle with breast cancer, Jewel continued to offer me insights that changed my view of the landscape and the dynamics of those who peopled it. She also provided me with advice, which I always welcomed even if I didn't always heed it. Some of my actions – including the Harvard protest leave – tried her patience, but she was never less than fiercely loyal. She resented deeply what she deemed Harvard's refusal to recognize my work, and finally accepted my leave-without-pay protest as a costly but necessary way of exposing the school's hypocrisy. Jewel died in early August of 1990, just before the start of the first year of my protest leave.

What Jewel brought to our marriage would have been valuable even if my ambition had been motivated by no more than the desire to maximize my income and status. But the challenge of an ethical ambition, particularly as I pioneered in new areas, would have been impossible for me without a partner who shared my commitment.

When Jewel died, I thought that my days as a life partner were behind me. A woman named Janet Dewart, who was communications director at the National Urban League, had different ideas. In fact, she proposed to me before we ever met.

She had read my work, and called for permission to republish one of my stories in the league's annual publication, *The State of Black America*, for which she was editor. I was happy to oblige her. Shortly afterward she sent for my approval an introduction she had written to the piece. I reworked it and sent it back, and in the following weeks we spoke about the piece and assorted other matters during what became almost daily phone calls. One morning, after about three months of these talks, Janet called and asked for my undivided attention.

She told me that, while we had not met, she felt she knew me well from my writings and our conversations. She said she believed in her heart that we cherished the same things, sought the same things, and strove for the same goals. We had both chosen careers that offered us the opportunity to do good in the world over careers that could offer us only money. We both believed in taking principled stands, even when we thought that we would not win the day. "I love you," she said, "and I think we would be very happy together." I didn't take her up on her offer immediately, but it didn't take me long to agree with her.

During our conversations, I learned that in addition to her leadership in community activities, Janet had taken part in the civil rights movement and had been arrested while protesting against the Vietnam War. She worked in and had a number of professional accomplishments in television, where her programming earned her an Emmy. Janet was one of the few blacks in broadcasting at a time when station executives, reluctantly responding to community demands, hired only a token number of blacks or women. While working for a D.C. television station, she refused a promotion to a position that was going to open once management fired another black woman whom Janet felt had been treated unfairly. "You can't refuse a promotion," she was told. "I can and I will," she responded. "What you are doing is wrong." "What happened?" I asked. "Neither of us was fired," she said.

Our marriage is now in its tenth year, and every day convinces me of how right she was. Important as we are to each other, our shared life is bigger than the sum of two individuals. Through our marriage, in ways large and small, we work to improve the world around us, each on our own path but providing ongoing support for our many projects.

Of course, marriage does not mean a trouble-free life. Just as the price of liberty is eternal vigilance, shared intimacy demands constant effort. For example, it assumes commonality of purpose, so when issues arise that reveal differences, reactions tend to be less tolerant than they would be if the same situation were to arise with a friend.

My good friend Phoebe Hoss likens intimate relationships to private institutions, with their own dynamics, and private and public functions and obligations. Ideally, it's a deeply enriching institution for both the couple and the public, as well as their circle of friends and colleagues.

Phoebe believes that the essence of love is a fundamental and continual attention to another, as well as to oneself – not giving way necessarily, but really learning to know each other while trying to work in mutual awareness. She feels most couples focus too much on what "I" need, which ends in polarization, and too little on what "we" need to keep viable the institutional work that they have undertaken.

Unfortunately, even a great many committed relationships run into serious difficulties that result in heartbreak and breakup. Even when they don't officially end, unhappiness is far more common among married people than the embodiment of fantasies of wedded bliss. Married people have to live in the world and are subject to all manner of changes and challenges that were nowhere on the horizon when they exchanged vows. Because a committed relationship is a living, breathing organism, those in it need to work at it. Marriage – and again I use the term generically – signifies a public manifestation of respect and commitment that most of us seek and even need, though many of us don't seem to recognize it. It is no exaggeration to say that an intimate committed relationship is the crucible of ethical action; we will always make mistakes, and there is always the possibility of learning from them, but if we cannot behave ethically overall toward the person with whom we have chosen to share our lives, what real value can there be in the show of ethical behavior toward others?

Sadly, the Achilles' heel of so many otherwise ethical people is their failure – seemingly an inability – to be sexually faithful to their partners. For those in positions of prominence, these dalliances – once merely whispered – are now bellowed from the virtual housetops, undermining their careers and bringing humiliation and pain to their partners and families. What can be called the "collateral damage" extends far beyond family. Even the most worthwhile projects in which the individuals are involved suffer a loss of confidence and respect. A former student, Lisa Boykin, expressed her pain and disappointment in straight-forward terms:

> When I think of so many prominent, married men who have sexual relationships and, in some instances, children with other women, how can I have respect for their moral authority and leadership given the way they treat their wives?

While the temptations to "cheat" may be great some-times, and the tacit approval of it seems to be all over our popular culture, there is very little to suggest that giving in to that temptation will bring more than a fleeting sense of happiness, if even that. Without intending to sound unduly moralistic, I can only say that if and when we feel the lure of romance or sex outside of the relationship we have com-mitted ourselves to, we would do well to ask ourselves if giving in to this is the sort of behavior we consider ethical.

Family is experienced in so many different ways (loving, inspiring, troubling . . .) that imagining it as revolving around the presence of children seems to suggest a sad lack of imagination. At the same time, even for those of us most vigorously committed to notions of family that may not include children at all, many of our most visceral conceptions of family are rooted in our experiences of parent-child dynamics. For most people, children are a principal reason for constituting family, if not *the* reason. It seems then that it should follow that a strong partnership relationship will almost guarantee happy, well-balanced children and wonderful interactions with family and relatives. The reality, of course, can be quite different, and a determination to live an ethical life brings its own challenges. This is particularly true of raising children, a universally humbling experience.

Jewel and I expected that if we could raise our three sons as firmly as we ourselves had been raised, they would inherit our values, and particularly our work orientation. Add to that the platform of our experience undergirded by income that placed them in good neighborhoods and good schools, and we believed they would take off and achieve heights beyond any we had reached.

As it turned out, parenting techniques that had worked for our parents were less effective for us, and quite possibly not appropriate. Our sons grew up in a world far broader and, in some ways, less nurturing than the one we had known. For one thing, I grew up in an environment where uncles, both real and adopted, aunts, and cousins were quasi-parents who offered counsel, rewarded my good grades with gifts, financed my various interests. They were family and they treated me as though I was very special. I grew up in one community where neighbors knew and respected my parents, and I benefited from being known as a child of Al and Ada Bell.

Our sons had more, traveled more, and even learned more from their reading than we had, not to mention what they learned from television. But instead of growing up in a single community, their childhoods were marked by our moves from New York to Washington, D.C., to Los Angeles to Cambridge to Seattle to Eugene, Oregon, and back to Cambridge. They got to attend better schools and live in much nicer homes than we did, but they had few extended family members to mentor and watch out for them, and nothing like the community that had given us a sense of place and belonging. We recognized this loss when they were young, with no certain means of meeting the challenge of getting our children beyond all the advantages we had provided them.

Being reminded that our offspring are God's children given us to nurture and guide is of scant reassurance when they show little interest in acquiring the credentials which in a credential society are almost measures of worth. Finding their own way meant that they ran info life's hard knocks, the very learning experiences we had hoped to help them avoid.

My sons are now in their middle to late thirties, and they are all good men whose company I greatly enjoy. Their work and their interests give them real rewards, and like their parents, they are more interested in well-being than wealth. They are sensitive to other people's feelings and needs — and always ready to reach out to help. I consider them a great blessing.

Although I spent substantial amounts of time with my sons as they were growing up, I was also away a great deal, particularly in their early years. Even when I was at home, the long hours I spent at my desk effectively rendered me unavailable to them, and certainly deterred them from considering careers in law. Whenever I suggested it, their response was, "No, Dad. You work too hard."

You work too hard. Four small words, but they packed a punch I didn't even know I was feeling at the time. As someone dedicated to the work of social reform and social change, I have found it difficult to say no to more projects; the no I didn't say usually translated into the sacrifice of time with my family. Such trade-offs become habit. Almost everyone on the trail of success knows the complaint about "living to work, rather than working to live." What is commonly called "workaholism" can become a serious neurosis, and yet those of us afflicted by it tend to see it as a virtue — we certainly do not view it as unethical conduct! Unfortunately, our passion for our work may be real, but carried to extremes it can result in our neglecting the people we care about most passionately. This, as Patrick J. Schiltz maintains, is both wrong *and* unethical.

Schiltz, now a law professor at Notre Dame, speaks from experience. Despite a fine law school record and a Supreme

Court clerkship, he turned down big money offers from big city law firms, and instead accepted a position in his home state, Minnesota, with a large firm that had a reputation for treating people well. Married and with a child on the way, he had every intention of leading a balanced life. Perhaps he did lead that life by the standards of New York or Washington law firms, but by anyone else's standards, including his own, he did not:

I worked three or four nights and one or two weekend days every week. When I was preparing for a trial or arbitration or appellate argument, I worked almost around the clock. I put hundreds of hours into business development, and, within three years or so, had created a self-sustaining practice. I traveled constantly. What I remember about the times my children first talked or walked or went to the potty was the hotel room in which I was sitting when my wife told me about the event over the phone. I was in Seattle when my grandmother died. I was in Pittsburgh when the worst snowstorm of the century trapped my family in our house for two days. I was in Williamsburg when my wife learned that our third child, with whom she was four months pregnant, had Down Syndrome. I failed miserably in my resolve to lead a balanced life, and neither my family nor I will ever be able to get back what we lost as a result.[23]

Professor Schiltz is quite open about the fact that, while he never thought about money before going into practice, slowly but surely making money became his chief goal. Finally he and his wife were able to recognize what had happened, and walked away from the money; he is now a full-time scholar and teacher. I would argue that the belief that you are working for justice and against evil can take over your life as much as the drive for wealth can. During my five years of litigation with the Legal Defense Fund, my hours and travel were the same as Schiltz reports working for his firm. I left for Birmingham less than an hour after our second child was born and was away in the South when our third child arrived – a friend had to take Jewel to the hospital. I was on the West Coast when the riots in Washington, D.C., broke out after the death of Dr Martin Luther King, Jr, and instead of being there with my wife and boys, I had to hear her describe the smoke and flames and mayhem over the phone.

To compound the damage done by the time I spent working, I was often in places where the white majority felt a palpable hostility for me and those with whom I worked, a hostility that could turn to violence in a heartbeat. My sons have to have understood that to some degree, and that knowledge has to have taken its toll.

Professor Schiltz and I were doing ethical work on the job, but we were both acting highly unethically with our families. Whenever I thought about it ("I should have been there, I should be there"), I rationalized that I was also sacrificing *myself* to long hours, and my family must certainly learn to bear my absence with understanding. They did, for the most part, but that did not make my work habits any less unethical. So, not surprisingly, my approach to working "as long as it takes" did not change as I took on other important jobs with the government, as head of a poverty law program in California, and then at Harvard Law. If anything, I worked harder.

Although she supported my work, Jewel reminded me more often than I like to remember that life was more than work. On occasion, I would agree and manifest my agreement by going to a movie or having friends over for dinner. But these were just breaks, rather than real changes in my work habits.

It would have required more insight than I had to recognize that while my work was important, my family was at least as important. They were entitled to more than my all-too-often long-distance love. What Professor Schiltz says about lawyers applies to people who work in many fields. He writes:

Being admitted to the bar does not absolve you of your responsibilities outside of work – to your family, to your friends, to your community, and, if you're a person of faith, to your God. To practice law ethically, you must meet those responsibilities, which means that you must live a balanced life. If you become a workaholic lawyer, you will be unhealthy, probably unhappy, and, I would argue, unethical.[24]

These words should be a flashing neon sign for the ethical person that courage can take many forms. For some of us, it is easier to confront an angry boss or even a hostile crowd than it is to leave an exciting work project and do justice as a spouse and parent. Achieving balance is an ongoing challenge, but an absolutely necessary one, and one well worth the continuing effort it requires. Work does have addictive qualities, but once away from my desk, I always enjoyed taking trips with my family or participating in any of the many activities that interested them.

And by the way, if you don't have children or a partner, don't think your relative solitude exempts you from this — if anything, since there's no one whose daily presence can remind you of the need for balance, you may need to be *more* careful to do your life justice.

While it's certainly possible that your good friends can have work habits as excessive as your own, friends can be a crucial component of a balanced life. How we choose and nurture those friendships can change dramatically depending on our maturity and our circumstances. When we are young children, we tend to make friends of the kids who live nearby in our building, or on the block. When we enter school our circles of acquaintance grow, but we still generally choose our friends from in our grade; as we grow older, we begin to make friend choices according to interest and temperament, but again our choices tend to be limited by our exposure and proximity, a pattern that can repeat itself well into adulthood.

Even for those of us whose circle of close friends is comparatively small, there is value in the companionship of like minds and spirits, and the challenges and joys that kind of companionship can afford us. Friends are the root of a sense of community; they are the people with whom we can share beliefs and experiences, often over longer periods than our family relationships. While it is difficult, I try to sustain close friendships over years and distances. For many of us, friends actually constitute family. And all of this can be enriched and complicated by a commitment to leading an ethical life.

But what about "*ethical* friendship" – what would that be? Is it only the obvious – you don't cheat your friend, borrow your friend's property or money loaned to you with no intention of returning it, or make passes at your friend's spouse? These are clearly basic ethical practices, but they do not sum up to the essence of ethical friendship. That, for me, can be done by the word "honesty." Honesty is a *sine qua non* for friendship and, in fact, any relationship worthy of the label "ethical," and this is a good moment for a brief comment about it.

Honesty is the core of all ethical relationships. Here, I am not talking about what Father Vincent Deer, my college ethics teacher, called "mental reservation," meaning there is no obligation to answer honestly questions about personal matters the questioner has no right to ask. Thus, when your spouse asks how you like the new outfit, a prudent rather than a coldly honest answer is appropriate. And when an acquaintance, out of the blue, asks about your sex life, you can say anything you want – or nothing at all.

However, when completing a job application, answering any question posed by officials, or in serious conversation with your spouse, family, and friends, tell the truth. It is not always easy; it can be difficult, discomforting, embarrassing, and humbling; in the worst of circumstances it can lead to trauma at home, dismissal at work, and humiliation in the community. There are times, in fact, when the truth feels unbearable and the temptation to lie is overwhelming – especially if we believe a lie will get us out of being caught in a *previous* lie.

This is how lying becomes a kind of voluntary servitude, requiring that we fabricate an alternative reality in a way that's absolutely plausible, and remember the difference between this reality and the "true" reality in case the issue comes up again (which it will). We then have to support that fiction with other fictions, and as if that were not enough, we have to remember which fictions we told to whom under what circumstances and why so we can be ready to improvise still *more* fictions to support them should circumstances require (which they will).

Telling the truth can be hard and even painful work, but lying, keeping the truth secret, is far more painful. When we think lying isn't hard and painful, it's rarely because it's become easy and pleasant; more likely it's because we have put up a wall between ourselves and our awareness of our captivity. This is why I am surprised that so few people in difficulty fail to tell the truth when confronted with conduct that is dishonest or less than honorable – even when admitting that conduct could lead to civil liability or criminal prosecution. Lawyers may advise clients to remain silent under constitutional protections. Generally, though, the truth *will* come out; when it does, chances are that you will be worse off for having dissembled, evaded, or out-and-out lied.

There is absolutely nothing like the truth. You deprive your enemies of most of their ammunition when you tell the truth. Your friends will usually forgive you and stand by you when you are forthright. It is always the best defense. Even a spouse devastated by what you have done will almost always rather know the truth than be deceived. In short, the truth can set you free. It is not simply the ethical thing to do. As with so many other areas, the ethical way is also the smart way.

Consider all the elected officials, including those at the

highest levels, whose terms in office were ended or seriously damaged because they insisted that they had not committed acts that eventually it became obvious they had done. Despite the temptations, despite the seeming safety in a secret or a lie, tell the truth. The connection between this and ethical ambition is obvious. Indeed, honesty is a key prerequisite of ethical living.

Over the years, I have realized a wonderful benefit through my efforts to treat my friends with honesty and integrity: It is my relationship with women. I have a number of close male friends, but thanks to the good fortune of having had a warm and compassionate mother, then marrying two wonderful and self-confident women, I developed relationships with women friends that have been extremely rewarding. There is much in our culture that confirms traditional notions of gender choices in friendship ("Hey, I love my wife, but I need to spend some time with the fellas . . ." or "My husband is my best friend, but there are some things you can only talk about with another woman . . .") and very little that encourages genuine friendship between men and women. I have always enjoyed the company of women who saw me not as a rival, suitor, or sexual predator, but as a friend. My experience is that when men show real interest in women as people whose company they genuinely appreciate – that is, when we behave ethically – we give women the freedom to drop the guard they often feel required to put up against the various kinds of assumptions and pressures they can get from men in so many different ways.

Another dividend of living an ethical life is the opportunity to serve as a mentor to students and others who recognize and respect your integrity and seek your advice on a range of problems and decisions. I benefited enormously from advice and wisdom I received when I was young and uncertain about my direction, and it is a privilege to pass on to others in payment for what I received. Having been on both sides of mentoring, I can say that it is one of the most genuinely pleasurable of the relationships I discuss here.

As a teacher, I believe that mentoring is part of the job, but I often go beyond giving advice about legal issues and job opportunities and respond to students about their personal problems. I regularly hear from former students who graduated years ago but want my views on a case or a career move. In a fundamental way, I see my writing as an extension of my teaching and mentoring, to a larger audience I could not otherwise hope to reach. Indeed, the principal rewards from my books have not been financial; they have come from my meetings with people who attend my readings and lectures, or even catch me on the street and ask me to autograph a dog-eared, heavily underlined copy of one of my books while telling me how much my writing has meant to them.

I am sometimes told that I should have remained at

Harvard because of the influence I could have had on the students admitted there. In fact, I often meet current Harvard Law students who tell me that they wish I were still there, but know why I left – and that they have read my books and profited from the reading. A teacher-mentor cannot hope for a more satisfying compliment.

I have not yet mentioned ways in which one's ethics can actually strain relationships; this is nowhere more true than in the workplace. While I believe I am outgoing and want good relationships with those with whom I work, the commitment to an ethical life can create divisions and distrust. As with family, we generally don't get to choose those with whom we work. And unlike family, we are rarely bound to working associates by a lifetime of knowledge and concern for their welfare and happiness. We might say in the broadest terms that we and our co-workers share a general purpose or a mission, but even this modest claim may be typically the exception, more honored in the breach than in the observance. More often than not we work in atmospheres where our particular function is so narrow that it feels isolated from the purpose of our organization or company or school or institution as a whole, and not much closer to that of the person in the next office or department or cubicle. In such an environment, the lack of connection we feel can make it more difficult to relate to working associates as human beings whose feelings and concerns are as real and as valid as our own.

But there is some consolation to be had here, because part of what makes it difficult to behave ethically in the workplace is also what makes it, in some ways, easier to resist actions that raise ethical issues. Although we may spend a large part of our waking hours with our co-workers, the fact that our whole lives are not bound up with theirs can offer us a clearer picture of what we believe to be right and wrong. The very limitations of our relationships with them can help us see more vividly – with less "emotional baggage" to muddy the waters – what actions are inappropriate and how we should react to them.

This is not to say that the workplace is some sort of ethics laboratory where we can perform experiments without ramifications. In fact, there have been times over the years when my efforts to live an ethical life have made me a poorer rather than a better colleague. I try to get along with everyone and pull at least my share of the workload, but my strong commitment to independence sometimes makes it hard for me to be a team player – particularly when the team wants to go in a direction with which I disagree. Sometimes this involves what I consider an ethical issue, but more often it is simply a disagreement. When I do go along, I try hard not to compromise my sense of independence.

My working career has exceeded all my early expectations, despite a determination to retain independence that is certainly related to racial concerns. It has not been easy to escape the fate of so many people whose lives were and are seriously circumscribed by varying forms of discrimination. Through struggle and my commitment to an ethical life, I have tried to overcome society's built-in impediments and achieved a large measure of personal independence. Beyond personal integrity, through, I realize that my hard-won ability to work through problems and implement approaches I think are ethical can often lead to giving little consideration to those, white or black, who disagree or urge a different course. My stance, I admit, makes it difficult for me to work for consensus on tough issues. In those cases I find myself more disposed to accept conflict than compromise.

I can see how this necessary defense mechanism has occasionally led me to give short shrift to the views and concerns of others. The Legal Defense Fund lawyers who told me it was too early to desegregate public schools in Mississippi were right. And, as I concede in the chapter on humility, my lack of vision convinced me that filing desegregation suits rather than supporting local leadership in nonlitigation strategies was the best way to help a Southern community gain a measure of racial equality. I was following the lead of others who believed deeply that our mission was right and our strategies would bring success. Even so, greater thoughtfulness, even in the midst of struggle, should be a component in the arsenal of the ethically committed.

Even back in law school where I was the only black in my

class, my single-minded determination to make it gained me a modicum of respect but few friends among my classmates. When a teacher asked another student a question, if the answer was not immediately forthcoming, my hand was waving in the air. The description under my photograph in the class book prepared at the end of the first year reflected what my classmates perceived as my lack of concern for the feelings of my classmates. It read: "Derrick Bell. Knows everything and wants everyone to know that he knows everything." I am sad to say that, at the time, I considered it a compliment.

Our relationships serve as our ethical barometers, and the ability to participate in meaningful personal relationships, intimate relationships, and relationships with family, friends, and colleagues is the cornerstone of ethical living. After all, what binds us is not blood, marriage license, or formal commitment, but pleasure, caring, and the trust that ethical behavior has earned.

CHAPTER FIVE

ETHICAL
INSPIRATIONS

The footprints made by the truly worthy,
far from intimidating, serve as models
for inspiration and emulation.

ONE OF THE great spirituals, probably best known as a
New Orleans jazz anthem, proclaims: "Oh when the
saints go marching in, Lord I want to be in that number,
when the saints go marching in." I have adhered to a
somewhat less ambitious corollary to the spiritual in that
I want to emulate those individuals who face great ethical
challenges and have stood their ground, had their say, and all
too often, paid a high price. I think they know or at least I
think they hope that when they make their controversial
statements, mount their unpopular protests, their courageous words and actions will serve as a model and will
encourage others to face challenges and defeats with the
same spirit and integrity.

At least since my college days, I have found inspiration in
such individuals and have wanted to be counted "in that

number." Following graduation from law school and after a quite short tour as a government civil rights lawyer, I returned to Pittsburgh to head the local branch of the NAACP. In addition to my administrative and fund-raising duties, I led efforts to integrate a public pool and a roller-skating rink on days other than the one day a week set aside for Negroes. I was inspired by the Montgomery Bus Boycott led by Dr Martin Luther King, Jr, but unlike Dr King, I often had difficulty imbuing my friends with the desire to do our part to desegregate public facilities in Pittsburgh. I learned that the way of the protester can be hard for reasons other than resistance by those determined to maintain practices of racial exclusion. My respect for those who inspired me was strengthened by experiences like one that taught me that my inspirations did not necessarily move others, at least did not inspire them to follow me.

For thirty minutes I stood on a downtown corner, waiting nervously for five friends to join me. I was wilting in the still oppressive heat of what had been a ninety-degree day. They had promised to meet me and their absence had me worried. True, I had reached the agreed upon meeting place just down the street from the Golden Triangle Bar (not the actual name) a few minutes before we were to meet at 6:00 P.M. As NAACP director and leader of the planned sit-in, I felt it was my duty to get there first.

It was all arranged. The date, the time, the place. We

would be well dressed in suits and ties, polished shoes with money in our pockets – just in case the general knowledge that none of the restaurants and bars in downtown Pittsburgh would serve Negroes was no longer accurate. It was, after all, 1959, five full years after the Supreme Court declared racial segregation in public schools unconstitutional. As in many cities outside the South, Pittsburgh's public facilities, restaurants, and hotels had no posted segregation signs – "white" and "colored." It was just understood. Negroes were not welcome and would not be served.

The Supreme Court's school desegregation case, of course, involved public schools, not privately owned facilities open to the public, but the stigma of racial rejection was just as keen, the continuing insult to every Negro just as hurtful. Similar protests were beginning in other parts of the country, North as well as South. Representing the NAACP, I could do no less than test the unofficial but no less rigid segregation in Pittsburgh.

Another ten minutes passed. By now, it was clear my friends who promised to join me in seeking service in one of the most popular bars in town were not going to show up. I could, of course, find a pay phone and try to reach them, but what could I say, "Hey, I'm here, where are you?" How could they respond other than with lame excuses to cover what they were already conveying by their absence?

Keeping your word regarding your promises and commitments, as I was learning standing on that street corner, is one of the more difficult aspects of an ethical life. It is so much easier to promise to do something you know you really should do, then, when the time comes to carry through, simply not show up. Did I really want to spend a warm summer evening testing the racial policy of an all-white, downtown bar? Of course not. I would rather be almost anywhere else, but I had promised to be there and not showing up would, for me, be more discomforting than standing there with perspiration from the heat and nervousness trickling down my neck.

Self-esteem is like a difficult-to-cultivate flower. It requires frequent nurturing that occurs when you keep your word and follow through on your promises – particularly when you would prefer not to function and simply offer excuses for nonperformance. A slight withering of self-esteem is the result, so slight that you may not notice because the next time you make a promise and then don't follow through, it seems a bit easier. And that's regarding the easy commitments. What I had asked friends from high school and college was not easy. None of us had tested the racial policy of a white bar before. Each man had promised he would be there. Perhaps, in this instance, regard for safety took priority over self-esteem. Whatever they were thinking, my philosophizing was not going to conjure them up.

I could call off the protest, regroup, and try again in a few days or a week, but I was geared up to test the bar this evening. I started walking toward the bar, all too aware that testing the bar by myself was imprudent, maybe even foolhardy. In a hostile environment, there was safety in numbers. But what the hell. I was born and raised in this town. Attended college and law school here, served the nation for two years as an Air Force officer, one of those years in Korea. I had every right to be served – whatever my skin color. If I was arrested or attacked, I could at least get some publicity for the local NAACP branch.

I entered warily, walking with as much confidence as I could muster. I climbed onto a bar stool, caught the bartender's eye, and ordered a Rolling Rock beer. He ignored me. I repeated my order. No response. The white patrons, deep in their conversations, acted as though I was not there. So, I sat and sat and sat some more with my blackness very visible, but intentionally invisible as a customer. I didn't have a backup plan for being ignored. How much more effective this test would be if with my friends we had occupied five or six of the dozen bar stools.

I considered demanding service in a loud voice, but it wasn't my style and management would call the police and have me arrested for disorderly conduct. Most of the patrons were businessmen. It was not a working-class bar where a more violent reaction to my presence would be almost certain. An hour went by. Customers came, drank, smoked, conversed, paid their bills, and left to be replaced by others. Some stared in my direction, curious, disdaining. No one spoke to me and the bartenders continued to refuse my periodically repeated orders. Another hour went by. It was getting dark and I saw a few young white men wearing T-shirts standing outside looking in the bar window. I decided it was time to leave.

"I am from the Pittsburgh NAACP," I said to the bartender. "We will be back." Then I walked out of the bar, ignoring the whites outside. One of them muttered, "Uppity nigger," but they didn't follow as I headed for the streetcar. Dressed as they were, they would have been no more welcome had they sought service in that businessmen's bar than I had been.

My effort had some benefit. At least at this bar, I had proved that the policy of not serving black people in downtown Pittsburgh was still in effect. I was angry about my treatment, and disappointed that good friends had not shown up to join me. At least, I told myself, I had taken the risk and gone ahead on my own.

Actually, I was back in Pittsburgh rather than still working for the Civil Rights Division of the Justice Department in Washington because of my respect for an early hero, William H. Hastie, a graduate of the Harvard Law School and the first black federal judge. Hastie had many accomplishments, but the inspiration he provided me was based on leaving an important government position when he recognized that he was being thwarted at every step and could not accomplish his goal of helping end segregation in the military.

During World War II, Hastie, hoping he might work from within, accepted a position as civilian aide to the secretary of war – one of the highest posts at that time held by any black person in the federal government. Hastie had doubts about accepting this position, worrying that he would be used to legitimize the segregation of black soldiers. That proved the case. He complained with little effect about military practices that subjected black soldiers to a steady barrage of racial epithets, violence, more severe punishment, and inferior facilities. Disheartened and realizing that he could neither end segregation in the military, nor make any of the major reforms for which he fought so determinedly, Hastie publicly resigned in 1943. Hastie's departure received front-page attention in the black press.

Likely unaware that I was more committed to the civil rights struggle than to keeping my job in the new Justice Department's Civil Rights Division, officials there probably felt it was no big deal when they told me that I must give up my NAACP membership because they considered it a conflict of interest with the civil rights work I was doing. Friends urged me to comply and work from within. I sought advice from by then federal judge William H. Hastie. I had met him while I was in law school and he praised my commitment to civil rights work. Hastie agreed with the friends who urged that as one of the few black attorneys in the Justice Department, I could remain, but he urged me to do what I thought was right.

My decision to resign was undergirded by my respect for what Judge Hastie had done years before. W. E. B. Du Bois lauded Hastie's action in terms that defined a standard of public performance in the area of social reform not limited to racial issues that, sadly, even today remains more the exception than the norm: He distinguished those who hold positions with impressive titles and no real power. They serve as apologists for the government's refusal to ease or even address racial issues. The other kind of race relations official, Du Bois said, tries hard to make progress and failing in the effort withdraws. Du Bois said Hastie belongs in this category – those who are useful and valuable.[25] I have never forgotten that distinction, but the line I have found is a thin one and easily blurred by ambition and the fervent desire to be a loyal team member when, in so many instances, a person, particularly a person of color, is not even considered to be on the team.

Were he alive today, Dr Du Bois would certainly place Congresswoman Barbara Lee among the public officials who are of "the valuable sort." Because the anger and the determination to seek revenge following the September 11, 2001, attacks was so great, her lone vote opposing giving the Bush administration broad war powers to fight terrorism would have prompted outraged criticism whatever her gender or race. And it did. The resolution, which authorized the use of force by President Bush in response to the terror attack, passed 98–0 in the Senate and 420–1 in the House.

Lee said she agonized before casting her vote and did so after sleepless nights and lengthy consultations with religious leaders, friends, and family members. From the floor of the House of Representatives, she warned a nation traumatized by attacks on the Pentagon and World Trade Center that "we must be careful not to embark on an open-ended war with neither an exit strategy nor a focused target." Just as important, Lee cited a prayer service at the National Cathedral honoring those who died in the attacks: "One of the clergy members said that as we act, we should not become the evil that we deplore."

Angered by her vote, people flooded Congresswoman Lee's office with angry phone calls, faxes, and e-mails, many of them threatening. Plainclothes policemen took up positions outside her Capitol Hill office. Even in her Ninth Congressional District, covering Berkeley and parts of Oakland, California, one of the most liberal in the nation, constituents held mixed views, seeing her vote as a "symbol of deep conscience, abject cluelessness, rare reason or misguided pacifism."[26] While a Democrat, Lee faced a reelection battle against challengers from both the Democratic and Republican parties. I have heard Congresswoman Lee speak and have marveled at her acceptance of the uphill fundraising effort she must make, crisscrossing the country to retain what should be a safe congressional seat. Not only is her courage inspiring, the reservations that motivated her vote have proved prophetic.

By the time of the California primary in March 2002, roughly six months after her "no" vote in Congress, a series of "War on Terrorism" actions by the Bush administration, as unnerving as they were far-reaching, led roughly 85 per cent of the voters in Lee's district to support her renomination.[27] While her victory was hardly mentioned in the media, Lee's stand is its own reward. It is a marvelous thing – and all too rare – that the rightness of her once-condemned action was publicly recognized during her lifetime. It is a dividend not often enjoyed by those whose primary ambition is a life of integrity.

My students have heard of and respect Congresswoman Lee. I recognize, though, that many of the individuals who inspire me with their courageous acts are mainly history for my students who were not even born when the events that I recount occurred thirty or more years ago. I can hear my students saying: "Professor, we also respect the individuals who risked and often lost a great deal as they fought against injustice. We see the risk taking, we see the sacrifices and suffering, but we don't see the connection between their lives and how we should live ours in this post-integration age." What I try to explain is that the individuals I admire – those on whom I have modeled my decisions and actions – were risk-takers in causes far greater than any of my ventures. And, I remind them, none of my protests was successful in bringing about the change I sought. Those who inspired me also failed to achieve the changes they sought. Through their example, though, I was able to recover from my setbacks on the issue, and feel triumphant in spirit.

Let me make clear that those whose stances inspire me are not what philosopher Susan Wolf calls "moral saints." I am not trying to emulate those who achieve fame because of their good works, but who are so single-minded in pursuit of their missions that they are lacking in personality, humor, and any serious intellectual curiosity beyond their work. In addition, my models have not all lived defect-free lives. They, like all of us, must reach beyond their shortcomings as they take on challenges against seemingly overwhelming odds.

During my years working in the Deep South, I was privileged to meet and work with many individuals who accepted the risks of their civil rights activities. I will never forget those nights I spent at Dr Aaron Henry's home in Clarksdale, Mississippi, deep in the Delta. Dr Henry, the state NAACP chairman, was outspoken in his condemnations of racism and, in response, was hated.

I slept on a couch in the Henrys' living room. Each evening at dusk, a gentleman would knock on the door and, when admitted, take his post in the living room's big front window, a shotgun across his lap. In the morning, he doffed his hat and left. I am ashamed to admit that I was nervous staying there because Dr Henry, his wife, Noelle, and their young daughter lived there through all those troubled years.[28]

I admired Dr Henry, but as he would agree, there was no more impressive civil rights advocate than Medgar Evers. A native of Mississippi, he accepted in 1954 the position as the first paid NAACP state field director in his home state. He traveled tirelessly around the state investigating lynchings and less fatal forms of intimidation. Later, as the civil rights movement reached Mississippi, he encouraged those who, despite all the obstacles and the risks, were determined to register and vote. He organized economic boycotts, and gathered petitions and information we needed to initiate civil rights litigation.

When there was a racial confrontation, Medgar was either at the scene or was on his way to help. During the three years I knew him, I was impressed by his calm and the ability to stay focused in the face of the dangers he considered a part of his job. Staying at his home as I sometimes did and having dinner with his wife, Myrlie, and their children, I marveled at their ability to maintain a sense of normalcy. And yet those determined to resist racial change in Mississippi considered Medgar Evers a serious enemy in what they considered an all-out war.[29]

In the spring of 1963, the NAACP mounted a series of protest marches and sit-ins challenging segregation in Jackson, the state capital. I was among several lawyers there planning and filing desegregation cases designed to end the exclusion or segregation of blacks in an array of public facilities. As expected, city officials resisted the campaign and over seven hundred protesters were arrested and jailed. Others were harassed as they sought service at white-only facilities. Medgar was everywhere during that hectic period. On a humid Saturday afternoon in early June, I joined him on his rounds. He spoke at meetings, identified possible witnesses for our cases, and offered reassurance to neighborhoods that feared trouble. We walked the streets together and Medgar, who knew everyone, was admired by everyone, offered friendly and encouraging words.

When I suggested canceling my trip home for the weekend so that I could offer legal advice he might need, he shook his head. "No, Derrick. You get back to New York and spend a few days with Jewel and your kids." I followed his advice and two nights later, our telephone rang late at night. Jewel answered and then handed the phone to me. I don't recall the caller, but I will never forget the message conveyed between sobs. "Derrick. Tonight, as he was getting out of his car in his driveway, someone shot Medgar from ambush. He's dead."

Medgar Evers met all the criteria for courage. He did not carry a gun and refused bodyguards. He was a man of peace and urged against violence in retaliation for violence. He loved Mississippi and his goal was to rid his home state of the racism that had defined and devastated both blacks and whites. His commitment to the dangerous work he was doing cost him his life at thirty-eight.

For about the first year of my work in the Justice

Department, I reviewed the appeals of men who sought to avoid military service into which they had been drafted by filing claims that they were conscientious objectors opposed to service in the armed forces. The exemptions from the draft under the Selective Service Law were quite limited, requiring that the refusal to serve in the military be based on sincerely held religious beliefs. Proof was not hard for longtime members of historical peace churches, like the Mennonites or the Quakers, but was much harder for others seeking exemption. I worked hard on these cases, fully aware that rejection of their appeals meant many of these men would be prosecuted and sentenced to up to five years in federal prison.

While I had no religious objections to military service and had gained an Air Force commission as a result of the ROTC training I received in college, I admired those men who filed these claims. Particularly during wars and times of crisis, there is little respect for those who refuse to serve, whatever their reasons. Stephen Decatur, a naval officer in the War of 1812, returning from a series of successful engagements in 1815, responded to a toast, stating: "Our country. In its intercourse with foreign nations, may she always be in the right. But our country right or wrong."[30] Whatever the wisdom of such ultranationalism, the majority of the country seems to adopt it during a war or serious international crisis. Under its unifying effect dissenting views are summarily dismissed as unpatriotic, even traitorous. Even those who have achieved wealth and wide-spread celebrity are brought low when they dare to criticize the nation's leaders and their war policies.

During the Vietnam War, a large number of men refused to serve because they were opposed to our military action in that particular war, a position outside the exemption requiring proof of opposition to all wars. Among the most famous resisters was heavyweight boxing champion Muhammad Ali. I admit that when he was Cassius Clay, while conceding his prowess in the ring, I did not admire his loudmouth boasting. I applauded his courage, though, when he announced: "I'm not going ten thousand miles from here to help murder and kill and burn poor people simply to help continue the domination of white slave masters over the darker people." When Ali refused to be inducted, he was stripped of his championship title and was not allowed to fight during this period. He escaped prison when his conviction was reversed on procedural grounds.[31] He regained his title and fought frequently. Even so, it was many years before his stance was recognized as courageous rather than unpatriotic.

The questionable history of some of America's wars does not diminish the "my country right or wrong" mania. Even civilian dissenters must expect and often experience little support and a great deal of enmity. I have never met Daniel Ellsberg, one of the many who became convinced that the American presence in Vietnam was wrong and was causing the deaths of thousands as well as the total destruction of a country. And I am far from sure that I would have had the courage to leak what became known as the Pentagon Papers, a voluminous set of classified documents which provided evidence that the government had lied to the public about its conduct in the Vietnam War. Ellsberg reports that during a year of intense soul searching before he released the material to newspapers, he found few people who believed that his proposed course of action was either prudent or likely to be effectual. Had I been in his shoes, my concerns would have broadened to include the significant danger for all blacks were I to have done what at the time was widely viewed as a traitorous act.

I met Dr Martin Luther King, Jr, and admired his work. I learned that he agonized and, because of the opposition of his staff and other civil rights leaders, vacillated for a long time before denouncing the Vietnam War. They warned that it would undermine his credibility and alienate the president and important supporters of the civil rights move-ment. Ultimately, he decided to speak up, and later ex-plained that he could not be silent about an "issue that is destroying the soul of our nation." He knew the cost of taking up this particular cross. He said: "The cross may mean the death of your popularity. It may mean the death of a foundation grant. It may cut down your budget a little, but you take up your cross, and just bear it. And that's the way I have decided to go."[32]

Dr King, of course, had been greatly admired and his courage was an exemplar for many long before he faced the Vietnam War crisis. I was inspired by his work in the Montgomery Bus Boycott that was launched in December 1955 when Rosa Parks refused to move to the back of the bus. I was in my second year of law school then and had made the law review. Enthused by the events in Mont-gomery, I began writing so many articles on racial discri-mination that the review's faculty advisor suggested – I think in jest – that I was trying to turn the magazine into the *University of Pittsburgh Racial Law Journal.*

Lacking a royal family, Americans often treat entertainers who attain star status as royalty substitutes. We follow closely every aspect of their lives and readily forgive all but the most outrageous of their shortcomings. When they voice poli-tically unpopular views, though, they are stripped of their regal status and become special targets. At that point, some of them stand up to their accusers and become for me inspirational models. It must require a special courage to confront for those who have spent their lives honing skills to entertain, to be accepted.

The communist witch hunts of the 1940s and 1950s, for example, seriously disrupted a number of professional ca-reers. Larry Adler, the harmonica virtuoso who brought his instrument to the classical music stage, was forced to live the remainder of his life in England after his support for nineteen

Hollywood writers summoned before the House Un-American Activities Committee. He claimed no interest in communist doctrine, but insisted that those who did had violated no law and should not be deprived of their ability to earn a living. Adler, in terms I have heard from others who have suffered for their stances, said he was not bitter about his political experiences, suggesting more than once that if he had to do it over again, he would have chosen the same course. "Resist the pressure to conform," he told young people. "Better be a lonely individualist than a contented conformist."[33]

Charlie Chaplin, perhaps the most famous of all the early film stars, fared no better than Adler. He achieved international fame and a great fortune with his portrayal of a pathetic yet humorous little tramp in American-made silent films. When his filmmaking turned to political subjects that were deemed critical of capitalist exploitation of workers, he was charged with being a communist. His films *The Great Dictator* and *Modern Times* raised questions about his politics with audiences who much preferred the icon of Chaplin as the tramp. Critics were able to twist his pleas for the common man into anti-American attitudes. His pledges of allegiance to international citizenship were construed as pro-foreigner zealotry. He was frequently questioned about his political views and his plea that "I am an artist, not a politician" was read as an admission that he was unwilling to confess his communist ties. In 1953, while in Europe for the premiere of his film *Limelight*, Chaplin, a citizen of Great Britain, was officially barred from reentry to the United States. Decades after the McCarthy era, he returned to receive a special Academy Award.[34]

Unlike Chaplin, Paul Robeson had neither a fortune nor a country other than America as a refuge. Along with millions of others, I admired Paul Robeson. Indeed, we named one of our sons Carter Robeson Bell. An all-American athlete at Rutgers, Robeson was a Rhodes Scholar and Columbia Law School graduate. He turned to the stage after experiencing racist rejection in the legal jobs he took after graduation from Columbia Law School. Robeson had enormous talent as a singer and actor and became the best-known and likely one of the highest-paid black men in the country. I still remember my parents, who did not go out often, getting all dressed up to attend a performance of Shakespeare's *Othello*, a controversial production in which Robeson starred as Othello and his Desdemona was played by a white woman.

He also had courage and fortitude equal to his ability as a performer. Robeson was likely as effective a civil rights warrior as any of the named heroes of the 1950s and 1960s. Ever the race man, Robeson devoted the last half of his life, in the pre–civil rights movement days of the 1940s and 1950s, to campaigning against the often violent manifestations of racism in this country. Taking on any and every injustice, Robeson worked to end lynchings, the Korean

War, Jim Crow laws, colonialism in Africa, and discrimination in immigration, in labor laws, and even in baseball,
among other things. In his career as a singer and actor,
he refused to perform anywhere the audiences were segregated.

Ignoring his agent's warning that he was doing himself "a
great deal of harm," Robeson risked everything and lost
everything. Refusing to temper his admiration of Russia,
where he had received good treatment at a time when
America's witch hunt for communists, not coincidentally,
tarred many of the country's most vocal critics, Robeson
was labeled a Party member and made an outcast. Towns
where he was scheduled to sing canceled his performances,
sparking a pattern that was to follow him across the country.
Radio and television stations, recording studios, and theater
and film companies barred Robeson entirely. His salary
dropped from over $100,000 to less than $6,000 per year. A
total pariah, Robeson was denounced in Congress, burned
in effigy, and threatened with violence. The government
had the FBI follow him, intercept his mail and his phone
conversations, and denied him the right to leave the country
unless he agreed not to make speeches criticizing this
country's racial policies. Robeson would not agree.

His career over and virtually alone, Robeson still refused
the government's insistence that he deny membership in the
Communist Party. In a hearing before HUAC in 1956,
Robeson stood on the Fifth Amendment and reiterated his

commitment to defending his rights, whatever the personal cost. When a senator derisively asked him why he did not live in the Soviet Union, Robeson responded: "Because my father was a slave, and my people died to build this country, and I am going to stay here and have a part of it just like you."[35]

The last years of Robeson's life were dominated by physical and mental illness. Severe depression, which caused him to try to take his life, confined him to mental institutions and then to his home. While unable to determine the cause of his illness, his doctors were never able to discount the adverse effects years of public hostility and hounding played in causing his poor health. Regrettably, Robeson likely heard too little of how much he was revered by working-class blacks, those who respect action more than position, defiant deeds more than fancy rhetoric.

I can't prove it of course, but Robeson's public criticism of racism in America may have played a major though unacknowledged role in the Supreme Court's 1954 decision declaring racial discrimination unconstitutional. Here was a black man, rich and famous, willing to sacrifice it all rather than remain silent about racial policies he thought were destroying the country. The justices surely knew about Robeson, and briefs to the Court made it clear that officially approved segregation in this country was harming our foreign policy efforts abroad. While not mentioned in the Court's opinion, media coverage of the decision made much of the fact that the decision would be of great value to our State Department.[36]

While a scholar and civil rights activist rather than an entertainer, W. E. B. Du Bois's experience was almost identical to Robeson's.[37] We named another son Douglass Du Bois. In his long life, Dr Du Bois was a modern Renaissance man. He was brilliant and courageously outspoken, a characteristic that made him as many enemies as admirers. Outspoken criticism of the U.S. government, particularly by a black man, is apparently particularly threatening. In his case, the government never gave up.

Du Bois was harassed by the government, tried and acquitted in 1951 when he was eighty-three years old on the charge of acting as a foreign agent, and had his passport withdrawn. In his own field, he could not find publishers for his writing or colleges at which to lecture. Also, like Robeson, he was abandoned, or worse, condemned by the mainstream black leadership. The NAACP fired him and later warned its branches to have nothing to do with him. I learned of his death at ninety-five in Ghana, Africa, while I was attending the famous March on Washington in August 1963. In both Robeson's and Du Bois's cases, though, their early fame resulted in a tardy but no less appreciative recognition of their courageous stands.

I readily admit that while I was inspired by the courage of Paul Robeson and W. E. B. Du Bois, the hostility they experienced frightened me. Nothing I have done has caused the government to launch the retaliatory attacks on me to which both men were subjected. My writings and speeches have been deeply critical of leaders of both parties. The attacks have not come, but they could. A few years ago, a law review article imagined that I had been nominated for a seat on the Supreme Court and, during Senate hearings, senators opposed to my confirmation quoted portions of my many writings. It was unnerving. All the quotations were accurate and I had meant everything I said. Were I to want Senate approval, I would have to try to water down and rationalize those writings.[38] The temptation would be great, but I would hope that the images of those who inspired those writings would come to the front of my mind, enabling me to defend those writings just as my inspirations stood their ground when their views were attacked.

Those who take strong positions contrary to government policy during wartime or other periods of national crisis can expect retaliation in one form or another. Persons working for corporations and institutions also face penalties when they refuse to follow the company line. Absolute loyalty as well as good work is expected of all those on the payroll. "Whistle blowers" is the rather derisive label reserved for individuals within an organization who, often after painful soul-searching, challenge those in charge by reporting unlawful, corrupt, or unsafe conditions they have uncovered on the job. Their actions are deemed traitorous, a condemnation that can be as damaging when leveled by a corporation as by one's country.

These individuals are not professional reformers. They hope to gain success in their jobs based on outstanding performance. They likely subscribe to the code that you owe your loyalty as well as your best efforts to those who hired you and pay your salary. They certainly did not imagine that their consciences would place them in uncomfortable and often dangerous positions. And yet, faced with choosing between loyalty to the organization and conscience, they choose conscience.

Dr Jeffrey Wigand, a high-level official of a tobacco company, decided that he could not join the tobacco industry's denials of the health dangers of smoking. Despite his highly paid, executive-level position, he agreed to testify both in court and on a nationally televised news program that his superiors had lied when they swore under oath at a congressional hearing that smoking does not cause cancer and other fatal illnesses. Somehow, Wigand withstood all manner of threats and intimidation intended to pressure him into silence. His testimony led to a major victory in court against the tobacco industry and his television appearance dramatically brought home to millions the addictive nature of smoking.

Wigand, though, lost his job and, unable to bear the coercion to which the family was subjected, his wife divorced him, taking their two children with her. Wigand became a high school teacher. Asked whether given advance knowledge of all that had happened to him, he would do it again, he, like others who have suffered serious loss because of their convictions, answered quietly and firmly that he would. Truly, these people are inspirational models to me. I may hail their courage without really understanding all the factors that motivated them to confront rather than conform, to risk the enmity of those in authority as well as the abandonment of friends and, sometimes, family.

The reprisals that a lone protester suffers are intended not only for the particular protester taking action, but also for those who would dare to follow them. Whatever form the expected retribution may take – loss of a job or the possibility of promotion, violence or the all too credible threat of violence – it is enough to keep many self-proclaimed sympathizers silent and on the sidelines. Perhaps most demoralizing is the well-founded fear that challenging authority will leave one isolated and alone, either politically or, more fundamentally, personally. It is only human to want to belong, to be a part of the group, "one of the gang." Because the solo protester risks both personal security and group identity, he or she also faces alienation from those who envy or resent the protester's willingness to take risks they cannot bring themselves to take. This resentment can manifest itself in a number of ways, none of them pleasant for the protester. Longtime friends simply drop out of sight or, when you see them, make no mention of your protest.

Sometimes, they join the criticisms of your opponents, although they insist that their harsh words are "only for your own good" or the good of your common cause.

My admiration for the persons I have discussed here heightens my efforts to emulate them and also to provide what help I can to those I know who are now under attack for their ethical stands. Professor Linda Bensel-Meyers, a rhetoric professor at the University of Tennessee, certainly merits what little support I can provide. She headed the university's tutoring program and for years complained to officials about the snap courses and easy grading she felt were cheating athletes out of a college education. She charged that compositions turned in by athletes were often written by the athletic department tutors, sometimes under coercion from the athletes themselves. She was ignored. After almost ten years of frustrated attempts to get an institutional response to the plagiarism and other ethical violations, in 1999 Professor Bensel-Meyers went to the media with her complaints. After her concerns were broadcast on ESPN, she began receiving plenty of attention in her sports-mad community, most of it hateful.

Immediately, Professor Bensel-Meyers became the enemy of Tennessee fans and coaches. While university officials steadfastly denied her claims and the NCAA has taken little action, opponents have inundated her with hate mail and threats of physical violence. To avoid angry and sometimes obscene comments, she no longer walks across campus and limits her trips to the mall. She doesn't work late at the office as she did previously, and when she drives, she stays on crowded streets, avoiding dark and unpopulated roads. People point from their cars, or drive beside her and threaten her. Leaving church where she plays the organ, sports fans stop to verbally attack her. Former lunch partners can't handle the fishbowl discomfort. Faculty members have apologized for their silence, saying they know that she is right, the university wrong, but feel that they must protect their jobs and families. She appreciates the few faculty members and friends who have stood beside her.

The controversy has led to the breakup of her marriage, adding to the misery she and her children are suffering. She is concerned about the adverse effects of her stance on her three teenaged sons. In an effort to get away from the hostility on her campus, Bensel-Meyers has looked for positions on other campuses, but after polite consideration, they tell her she would not fit in or that they have decided to give the position to another candidate. The Tennessee Volunteers jackets she used to buy no longer dot the house. "There's a lot of betrayal behind it," she says of the beloved orange. "It's exploitation. To celebrate all the merchandising behind it is to exploit the athlete. And I can't be part of the exploitation . . ."[39]

For more than a year, Professor Bensel-Meyers and I have communicated via e-mail at least a few times each week. At times, her despair is as deep as her situation at the university is dire. I am inspired by her stance even as I try to offer support for what she is going through. Again and again, though, she rises to the occasion. In one e-mail, she wrote:

> I've got to remember to feel good about exercising my freedom to follow my own conscience at each step of the way, and to see any retaliation as merely others' attempts to justify their choices. Although there are no fast and eternal answers for how we should act at any one time to competing responsibilities, bumbling along as we humans do, freedom is the effect not the cause of always acting on the principle that everyone is free and equal. "It is the cause" that motivates us, not the result; and everyone has only their own perception of the "cause" for why they do what they do. All I can hope is that by keeping "equal access" in the vocabulary, it will by necessity remain potentially there.[40]

Professor Bensel-Meyers stands with the legions of ordinary people who without wealth, position, or prestige risk everything they have to protect their sense of integrity when they oppose injustices to themselves and to others. While not acting out of any hope for acclaim, most suffer their ordeals unknown and unappreciated. At bottom, their actions give meaning to folk singer Tracy Chapman's song, "All That You Have Is Your Soul."

154

CHAPTER SIX

HUMILITY'S WISDOM

Self-righteousness is a gentle curse visited on those
striving for social reform and personal uprightness.
Humility, no cure, can serve as a continuing
reminder of the difficulty of doing good.

B Y THE EARLY 1970s, school desegregation battles had
moved North. After years of bitterly contested litigation in Boston, the federal court was ready to order black
children into white schools in lower-income areas, including South Boston, where hostility toward blacks had festered
for generations. In a meeting with civil rights lawyers
handling the case, black community leaders made it clear
that parents did not want to send their children into white
schools where they would be in danger, and where the
educational standards were worse than those at the mainly
black schools their children now attended. The lawyers —
most of them black — listened politely, then told the
community leaders that the law required and they would
seek orders sending their children to white schools whether
or not parents wished them to go. As the community leaders

feared, the desegregation that followed was both dangerous and traumatic for the black children who were bused to white schools.

The civil rights lawyers meant well. They knew that school desegregation would be difficult, but saw it as the only way to ensure better schooling for black children. And, they were convinced, it was the only route to an integrated society. Unfortunately, their optimism was based less on evidence than wish, and a generation of children paid the price for that error.

By the time of the meeting, I was teaching but had been invited to attend the meeting with the lawyers by the black community leaders. I disagreed strongly with the advice the lawyers provided and voiced my objections, but nothing I said convinced them to reconsider their plans.

Sitting there, I realized that my anger at the lawyers' rigidity and insensitivity to the black community's quite justified concerns was fueled in part by guilt. Not too many years earlier, I had been in their shoes and given hosts of parents and community leaders quite similar advice. When I worked with the NAACP Legal Defense Fund and the federal government, I labored mightily to desegregate public schools across the South. I too was committed to achieving racial balance as the best means to desegregate schools. And I too was insufficiently sensitive to how much would be lost when black schools were closed with most of the black teachers and principals dismissed. Worst of all, I knew that black children and their parents would have to seek the equal educational opportunity we lawyers promised them in often hostile and always alien schools that remained dominated by whites. I rationalized that this was the necessary price for moving school systems away from their long-held "separate but equal" policies.

As the Boston meeting continued with voices raised in anger and frustration, my mind went back to a Deep South federal courtroom where an incident raised doubt as to the wisdom of our school desegregation policies. It was my fourth year at the NAACP Legal Defense Fund. I was supervising three hundred school desegregation cases all across the South and was convinced that I was doing God's work. I knew the economic and even physical risks being taken by the parents of the children we were representing. Many had joined the cases at our urging, and despite their concerns. They were willing to risk a great deal to give meaning to what the Supreme Court had said was their right back in 1954: effective public schooling for their children. But now, a decade later, segregated schools remained the rule all across the South. The significance of this fact was brought home by what I had just seen in the courtroom.

The hearing on our school desegregation case had been delayed yet again, this time because the judge wanted to administer the oath of citizenship to a group of white immigrants. Even though the law was clearly in our favor, this member of the federal judiciary had been particularly resistant to our suit, treating us and our clients with contempt (turning away from us to face the wall when we spoke, overruling every one of our objections), while allowing the school board numerous delays, and letting the board's lawyer introduce all manner of irrelevant testimony and materials.

But moments ago the judge underwent a total change of demeanor. He asked the newly minted citizens to gather around the bench to be sworn in, then welcomed them to the country in tones of sweetness and warmth that were the Dr Jekyll opposite of the Mr Hyde treatment he'd been giving my clients for seeking the relief to which *the Supreme Court* had said they were entitled a decade earlier.

But that wasn't what surprised me. What froze me in my seat, dumbfounded, was this realization: The moment these people became citizens, their whiteness made them more acceptable to this country, more a welcome part of it, than the black people I was representing would likely ever be. The realization pushed me to a moment of existential doubt: What was the point? Why was I trying to get children admitted to schools where they were not wanted and where – unless they were exceptional – they would probably fare poorly? Chances were good that they would drop out or be expelled for responding with anger or violence to the hostile treatment they were sure to receive. So what was I doing?

The courthouse epiphany rocked me. I believed that

these cases were a legally necessary if not a very efficient means of giving black children effective schooling. I continued my work in school desegregation, but with a growing sense that the symbolic value of eliminating dual school systems was not equaled by substantive educational benefits for our clients, or the millions of people they symbolically represented. I had been humbled by reality, and while at first I worried that this was a flaw in the idealism I needed to do this work, I soon understood that humility is a crucial kind of strength.

A troubled conscience is a worrisome thing, but it is an indispensable component for a person committed to any area of social reform work. You might think it should be enough that resistance is usually great and progress almost always painfully slow. However, those who work to effect social change through ethical means must constantly review the actions they themselves take on behalf of others. Power in the hands of the reformer is no less potentially corrupting than in the hands of the oppressor. My friend the Reverend Peter Gomes expressed this concern in a very usable formula. He was speaking at a dinner the black students at Harvard were giving me before I left to accept the deanship of the University of Oregon Law School.

"Derrick," he said, "as a dean, you must look in the mirror each morning and say, 'I am a dean and thus I am an evil.'" We all laughed, but he went on to explain. "As dean, you will have authority over many others; sometimes you will disappoint expectations you should reward; sometimes you will reward expectations you should disappoint. Try as you might, there is no way you can avoid such mischief. So each morning upon arising, you must look in the mirror and remind yourself, 'I am a dean and thus an evil.' Then you must promise, 'But today I will try to be a *necessary* evil.'"

In a matter of weeks, I learned that the good reverend had overestimated the authority of a law school dean – for either good or mischief. His admonition, though, is quite appropriate for those involved in efforts to end discrimination, exploitation, and general social injustice. We need to look in the mirror frequently and remind ourselves that our good intentions, even when supported by impressive skills and hard work, do not endow us with either the certainty of victory or any perfect sense of what those for whom we labor will consider victory.

I cannot emphasize enough what I see as the potentially dangerous and destructive consequences of words and actions intended to do good. Medicine has long had the term "iatrogenic" to describe conditions accidentally caused by the doctor, whether through treatment, diagnosis, or even manner. We might say that, as with the healing arts, so with the practice of those of us who seek to heal the bodies politic, social, and economic. It is the most frequently ignored pitfall of those motivated by good intentions, particularly those involved in social change and progressive politics. Without a willingness to continually critique our own policies, question our own motivations, and admit our own mistakes, it is virtually impossible to maintain programs and practices that are truly ethically related to the real needs of those we wish to serve. As I learned from sad experience, it is all too easy to become so committed to ideals and goals that we fail to notice when our clients' interests and goals no longer coincide with ours.

"Fail" is usually a painful word in any context, but let's consider it for a moment and contemplate how a notion of failure might serve us well. So many times when people consider movements for social justice, it is with a taste of the bittersweet because no matter how mightily (and even, to some degree, successfully) we strove to see justice triumph, we are still dealing with the very things we hoped to see disappear: racism, poverty, homophobia, sexism, classism, and elitism. I am convinced that these social injustices, while changing in form, will remain a permanent part of the landscape until far more people realize that the subordination of other people serves as a major barrier to their own ability to move up the economic ladder. But does this prove that all the attempts, large and small, to combat these injustices were failures? Absolutely; and absolutely not.

Ethical actions must always fail if we understand them in terms of end goals: The fight for women's suffrage and the passage of the Nineteenth Amendment did *not* make women equal citizens. After a half-century of effort, most black children still attend schools that are mostly black and, in all too many instances, mostly unequal. Despite the fact that some forty million Americans lack health coverage, the effort to achieve universal health insurance remains a goal blocked by seemingly impassable obstacles.

The constant change inherent in human life, and the glacial pace of institutional change, almost assures us that no dramatic change – no matter how fully and deeply con-ceived or enacted – is likely to achieve even most of what it promises; if your criterion for success is perfection, then the failure of every ethical action is assured. We also bind ourselves to a notion of failure when we ourselves refuse to change, or can't acknowledge change that's happening.

There's a Buddhist saying to the effect that you need a raft to cross a river, but once you've crossed you don't keep the raft with you. Because the struggle to improve conditions for people without money or power is so tough – like crossing a very swift-running river – those making the effort burden themselves by equating commitment with a rigid adherence to policy positions that may have worked at one point, but because of changed conditions are now no longer effective. Reform organizations and their leaders become identified with pursuing change through a particular set of tactics. We reason that we are in the right, that the forces we oppose are in the wrong, and any deviation from policies adhered to over many years will be seen as lack of commit-ment, or a concession that we were wrong all the time.

The decades-long campaign to ensure choice for women is a prime example. Along with many others, I hailed the Supreme Court's 1973 decision in *Roe v. Wade* as giving poorer women the choice whether to carry their pregnancies to term that better-off women have always been able to exercise. Some pro-choice advocates believed that a Supreme Court victory guaranteed the defeat of anti-abortion forces and formed the legal basis for ending all injustice against women; just as many who were committed to racial integration had believed the same about the defeat of segregationists and the end of injustice toward blacks.

Faye Wattleton, the former president of Planned Parenthood, recalls that shortly after *Roe v. Wade*, political guru David Garth gave pro-choice advocates a warning: "The Supreme Court decision did more than just legalize abortion; it neutralized you, it robbed you of your rallying cry, your most provocative issue, your activist identity."[41] To counter this, Garth urged Planned Parenthood to broaden their political platform and strategies, but they rejected his recommendation. The anti-abortion forces, on the other hand, energized by the decision that went against them, *did* become politically active, and played a pivotal role in the political landscape of the next generation.

The point of this is not that those who worked hard to bring choice to all women were misguided, any more than those who fought for integration were wasting their time. But what the pro-choice movement had in common with

the movements behind school integration, affirmative action, the Equal Rights Amendment, and so many social
reforms championed and eventually defeated, is the effort to
shoehorn essentially economic and class issues into constitutional norms, neglecting the structural protections of
vested wealth that keep so many people living so poorly
in the world's richest country. The longtime focus on law
often ignored the political dimension, including organizing
those we wish to help for political leverage and direct protest
activities. Perhaps the wisdom we have collectively achieved
from reflecting on some of these oversights of judgment can
combine with humility to help us think and strategize more
flexibly and effectively in the future.

I do not believe that earlier attempts to combat social
injustices were failures, even if they did not realize their
goals, or once achieved, proved of only temporary value. I say
so harking back to our discussion of faith and remembering
this: If our goal is greater than ourselves, our own comfort or
gain, and we continue to strive for it, then as feminist leaders
proclaimed, failure becomes impossible. Even the end of an
individual life is no proof of failure, if others share your goals
and continue to work toward them.

In effect, then, failure is inevitable, and there need be no
failure. If we can acknowledge that what we might think of
as "the perfect good" – one in which everybody benefits
and no one is deprived – is not possible, then everything we

achieve short of perfection is a good. Beyond this, the degree to which our achievements fall short of perfect is the degree to which they can teach us humility. And this humility – the acceptance of inevitable failure and the willingness each day not to be daunted by it, the conscious connection of our knowledge and our experience – is perhaps the last key to ethical action, an element without which action cannot long be ethical.

Humility gives us space to see that we do not have all the answers, even in our so-called areas of expertise; it lets us listen and respond to what is actually happening, being said, being felt.

My goal is to inspire and encourage people to achieve their full potential while simultaneously affirming for them and with them that the road they travel to success is often filled with barriers placed by a society that relies on inequality for stability. A national awakening on these issues will not come easily, but it is a worthy goal to which individuals and groups as well as elected officials can devote their efforts. As reform takes place, there will be less temptation to live unethically and, one hopes, plenty of motivation to measure success by efforts to do right by others, which, as all will realize, is the only sure way to do well by yourself.

Idealism need not require the abandonment of realism. If we subjected social reform programs and projects to serious scrutiny, I wonder how many we would see as sensible let alone relevant, given the powerful dynamics that can transform even our social reform victories into new forms of disadvantage. Litigation and legislation intended to ensure fair trials, fair sentencing, and humane prison facilities has achieved little to none of the above. Government entities respond to our hard-won procedural safeguards with cutbacks in services that worsen the plight of those trapped in the already beleaguered criminal justice system.

In each of these areas — and many others as well — campaigns to attain or further what we consider "good" have proven costly when they failed, and counterproductive even when their original goals were achieved. What is the component in so many of our social reform strategies that transforms even the most committed effort into futility, frustration, and failure?

If I had a solution or even a responsible theory to address this difficulty of doing good, the dilemma facing both individuals and groups seeking, as Dr King put it, to "let justice ring," I would have reported it long before now. I can offer only a rationale for continuing the struggle even in the face of almost certain failure. This rationale is connected with the reason that so many pursue wealth and the rest of us persist in our justice quest — even with knowledge (albeit mostly suppressed knowledge) that the reasons we offer for our pursuits and persistence will not stand (and thus does not often receive) what we in the law refer to as "strict scrutiny."

It is time that we face up to the difficulties of doing good as we work for social reform. Those difficulties need not deter but should give us reason for humility as we pursue programs that no matter what we do are likely to wither under the pressure to continue the injustices we are trying to end. Indeed, humility should be the watchword for social reformers. It is amazing how things said, actions done, even with the most helpful of intentions, can serve to make a bad situation worse.

It is not easy to look back over a long career and recognize with some pain that my efforts may have benefited my career more clearly than they helped those for whom I have worked. It took me far too many years as a civil rights lawyer before I learned to listen carefully to those I wished to help. And, in listening, we must not do them the injustice of failing to recognize, as we empathize, that somehow they survived as complete, defiant human beings. We must learn from their example, learn from those whom we would teach; be humble, and emulate them.

The affliction of all activists is the knowledge – usually painfully gained – that there are no unmitigated good works. Each action intended to help some will unintentionally harm or disadvantage others, who, as a result of our well-intended efforts, will feel – and may well be – less well off. There is no solution to this, the ethical activist's dilemma, a dilemma that affects and can afflict every aspect of life for those not involved in social reform. A wise humility is valuable in our relationships with others, particularly life partners and their children. The passion we bring to our work, the risks we undertake to oppose wrongs confronting us or others, our manner as we explain our religious beliefs, all will benefit from a leavening of humility. It can lessen our regret when the world proves different than we thought without restricting our joy when events affirm the wisdom of our advice, our actions.

The admissions of past error and present inadequacy make it possible to accept the well-intended praise of those wishing to commend our efforts to serve others. They offer a value beyond commendation. It is reassurance. But there is a balm for its pain in the recognition and encouragement from neutral observers who – we must assume – have seen the big picture, have weighed our good intentions against any evils we unleashed, and found us, there is no better word, worthy.

CONCLUSION

Good counsel is all too often the product of hard-earned experience.

THE GNOSTIC GOSPEL According to Thomas contains a passage in which Jesus is reported to have provided the following wisdom:

If you bring forth what is within you,
What you bring forth will save you.
If you do not bring forth what is within you,
What you do not bring forth will destroy you.[42]

I had not read and recognized in this quote a potential answer to a question Jewel asked when I told her I planned to take an unpaid leave to support the students' months-long protest against Harvard Law's failure to ever hire a woman of color for its faculty. Already quite ill with the cancer that would claim her life within four months, she asked: "Why does it always have to be *you*?"

She hoped – not for the first time – that a question from

her would move me to scrutinize my actions, maybe even reconsider them. She knew the pattern: I would resign or launch a risky protest – usually on my own – that would seldom change the condition I deemed wrong or unjust. My action almost always upset those in authority and usually alienated working associates who saw my solo actions as not only futile and foolish challenges to those in authority but as possibly jeopardizing *their* far from stable place in the status quo. And they always had their own question to ask, in one way or another: "Who do you think you are?"

Our friends were aware of Jewel's failing health, and I fear some of them have never fully forgiven me for going ahead with the protest. One called and said, "For God's sake, Derrick, think of your wife." I did think of her, constantly. I knew she was not happy about the protest, but I think – I hope not selfishly – that canceling my plans because she was so ill would have been even more upsetting to her. Those two questions – *Why does it always have to be you?* and *Who do you think you are?* – are the kernels of the themes with which I have wrestled in this book.

I have always had a clearly perceived if not carefully examined need to stand up and articulate my opposition to wrongs taking place around me. When I was a child, my inner motivation was nurtured by my parents and extended family members who treated me as someone very special. As a young lawyer, I had the example of committed excellence provided by Thurgood Marshall, Robert L. Carter, Constance Baker Motley, and the many lawyers living in the South who risked their livelihoods and often their lives to handle civil rights cases that were anathema to the larger communities in which they practiced their profession. And then there were my clients, average people often with quite modest incomes whose courage in joining our suits and whose commitment to changing a system that had worried their days and diminished their lives I witnessed with insufficient appreciation.

The challenges I've faced throughout my life, the examples of so many people who have shown a commitment beyond my understanding, have motivated me to prove to myself that I could defy stereotypes and follow roads less traveled. Were the barriers of race and class set by others a good thing? Of course not. They were simply there, built into the playing field that I have worked to level. Nonetheless, they created a clear and consistent enemy against which I could attempt to build a life of excellence and achievement. In this sense, every obstacle became an opportunity to challenge what I deemed evil and, at the very least, not acquiesce in allowing that evil to become a destructive force for me.

For members of oppressed groups and for progressive thinkers of all backgrounds, resistance is a powerful motivator precisely because it enables us to fulfill our longing to achieve our goals *while* letting us boldly recognize and name the obstacles to those achievements. It motivates us to resolve our ambivalence about success by giving us a reason to succeed that is embedded in a history of the struggles, social and personal, that have made success possible for us. Resistance-motivated success – ethical success – allows us to balance our desires and our beliefs. And this balance gives meaning to our work and substance to our lives.

One of the most powerful ways by which we can resist the temptations all around us is by maintaining a stance that reminds us and shows others how much more we are than simple adherents to whatever the current consensus happens to be. We move beyond the popular and let the "in crowd" go its way. We look instead to those who love us for support *and* criticism. We rely on faith in a power or cause that surpasses understanding to sustain us. With this foundation, we achieve our successes, when we do, with moral and political integrity; with this foundation, our successes become not just personal triumphs but victories for our entire communities.

The predictable outcome of efforts for human justice across history has been built on courageous manifestations of faith far more than preachments or promises. It has required a commitment to a cause and an engagement in that commitment quite like that so many black people in America have been doing since slavery: making something out of nothing. Like the dispossessed in all times, these individuals carved out a humanity for themselves with absolutely nothing to help – save imagination, will, and unbelievable strength and courage. Beating the odds while firmly believing, knowing as only those who are the disinherited of their societies can know, that all those odds are stacked against them.

This is a philosophy of life that is easier to praise than to emulate. It is an outlook perhaps only available to those with the always hard to accept perception that life is a gift that can be revoked at any time and that, at some point, will come to an end. And at that end, we know our work will not be completed. Perfection will have evaded us as it has for all who came before us. If there is satisfaction, it must come from our striving toward that vision of a better world. When I was recovering from a life-threatening case of viral pneumonia a few years ago, a doctor reviewed my medical chart, shook his head in astonishment, and told me, "As far as your life is concerned, you have gained a stay. Use it well." We both smiled at the significance of his observation.

Actually, all of life is a reprieve, a fact we acknowledge with reluctance. It is this quite human fear-motivated denial of the inevitable that Morrie Schwartz addressed in the Mitch Albom book, *Tuesdays with Morrie*.[43] In one conversation, Morrie, suffering in the last stages of Lou Gehrig's disease, tells his former student, Mitch:

Everyone knows they're going to die, but nobody believes it. If we did, we would do things differently . . .

There's a better approach. To know you're going to

die, and to be *prepared* for it at any time. That's better. That way you can actually be *more* involved in your life while you're living.

Morrie Schwartz's observation has value for all of us, including those so sure of life that they risk death in dangerous recreational activity in a continuing quest for excitement. Recognition of life's impermanence can also lead to despair, but for those trying to live ethical lives, the effort can provide insulation against the desires and lusts and foolishness of our world. It enhances the willingness to fight on in good causes, ignoring those who maintain that we are wasting our time.

What I find life affirming through the conscious acknowledgment of its evanescence is the clarity it offers us as ethical people: the awareness that there is always more good work to do than there is time or energy in which to do it. Here is a much-needed sense in our hedonistic world that enables us to choose the good over the feels-good. Not always, certainly not every second, but often enough to become a habit of life that nourishes rather than diminishes us. This is a sense of urgency that has nothing frantic to it – in fact, the clear sight it offers us has the effect of making our choices easier.

There is another awareness, directly related, that has a similarly salutary effect. Along with the understanding of our own mortality – how fleeting health and strength and life can be — a knowledge that what we do affects the lives of those who come after us can equally inform our sense of duty. It's certainly possible to lead a solipsistic life, one that boasts, "Hey, I'm making it real. Who's it going to hurt?" This mentality allows us to think our actions and inactions take place in a vacuum, but even the faintest conscious sense of our infinite interconnectedness makes that almost impossible. The more we consider the world we will leave behind us, the more we can use that consideration to motivate right choice and right action. Every parent has probably had a thought along the lines of "Well, if it were just me I'd . . . but I've got my kids to think about." Extend this thought to "but I've got everyone who comes after me to think about," and any notion of a life given over completely to self-satisfaction is likely to taste very sour very quickly. Whatever we do, there is another generation waiting to learn from our legacy. It is they who must live in the world we make.

Here is the foundation of Professor Patricia Williams's response to the intellectual critics who asserted that it is foolish for black people to persist in their quest for rights. She concedes that the concept of rights is indeterminate, vague, and disutile. She readily acknowledges, moreover, that the paper promises of enforcement packages like the civil rights acts have held out as many illusions as gains. She recognizes, as well, that blacks have never fully believed in constitutional rights as literal mandate. Despite all these concessions, she rebuts and likely confounds her critics in terms that constitute as much creed as response:

> It is also true that blacks always believed in rights in some larger, mythological sense – as a pantheon of possibility. It is in this sense that blacks believed in rights so much and so hard that we gave them life where there was none before; held onto them, put the hope of them into our wombs, mothered them, not the notion of them; we nurtured rights and gave rights life. And this was not the dry process of reification, from which life is drained and reality fades as the cement of conceptual determinism hardens round, but its opposite. This was the story of phoenix; the parthenogenesis of unfertilized hope.[44]

It is an explanation that transcends understanding and rises to the status of prophetic insight. It acknowledges the harsh truth that life seems to favor those in power, while it seldom rewards good works with triumphs. As James Russell Lowell put it: "Truth forever on the scaffold. Wrong forever on the throne."[45] Defeat, disgrace, and sometimes death are often the fate of the righteous who must rely on their faith that truth and justice were worth championing, even in a lost cause.

It is both necessary and reassuring to question what we do as we continue doing something. We cannot know whether our actions are a help or a harm. And that, of course, is not the test. Our lives gain purpose and worth when we recognize and confront the evils we encounter – small as well as large – and meet them with a determination to take action even when we are all but certain that our efforts will fail. For in rising to those challenges, there is no failure. Rather there is the salvation of spirit, of mind, of soul.

Keep in mind, activism does not equal martyrdom. Some activists have certainly been martyrs to their causes, and we appropriately give them our attention. They merit our respect. They are, in most times, the exception, not the rule. It thus bears repeating: an ethical life is not a life of sacrifice. It is, in fact, a life of riches. The riches may not always, or even often, be material, but the satisfaction of choosing ethically enriches the fabric of our daily lives in ways we might otherwise have thought impossible. The many ethical people it has been my blessing to know generally lead lives that are satisfying – even as they face almost daily challenges, frustrations, and dissatisfactions. An activist life, an ethical life, is more often than not an adding to, not a taking away.

In other words, we can be ambitious, strive for success, if our ambition is powered by a passion for the good and the just that may include your personal comfort but goes far beyond it. Let our sense of success be far broader and deeper than us and our kin. Let it inform the choices we make, big and small, public and unseen. We need not aim for sainthood, but by striving to choose ethically – no matter the "success rate" – we will have a cumulative wealth of knowledge and experience to draw on and pass on that will pay dividends throughout our lives and beyond. Through our choices, day by day, we will be the success we aim for.

Here is the essence of Dr W. E. B. Du Bois's message to two thousand friends and well-wishers who gathered at the Roosevelt Hotel in New York in 1958 to celebrate his ninetieth birthday. Moved as he must have been, Du Bois used the occasion to convey a legacy to the audience and to the world in which he had been so actively involved. Noting the presence of his great-great-grandson, only a few months old, Du Bois said:

You will find it the fashion in the America where eventually you will live and work to judge life's work by the amount of money it brings you. This is a grave mistake. The return from your work must be the satisfaction which that work brings you and the world's need of that work. With this, life is heaven, or as near heaven as you can get. Without this – with work that you despise, which bores you and which the world does not need – this life is hell . . .

Income is not greenbacks. It is satisfaction, it is creation; it is beauty. It is the supreme sense of a world of men going forward, lurch and stagger though it may, but slowly, inevitably going forward, and you, you yourself with your hand on the wheels. Make this choice, then, my son. Never hesitate, never falter.[46]

ACKNOWLEDGMENTS

T HERE IS SOMETHING especially gratifying about writing a book that becomes a collaboration with others who believe in your vision and help bring it forth. I must start off by acknowledging my agent, Tanya McKinnon of the Mary Evans Agency, who took interest in an unpublished memoir and over many patient months convinced me it was the basis for this book. As our excitement about this new work grew, Tanya recruited her friend, Dionne Bennett, who suggested the title.

The circle of collaborators – people who offered advice or otherwise contributed to the depth and texture of the book – are: Kathy Bergin, Rev. Gail Bowman, Lisa Boykin, Sheryll Cashin, Jean Fairfax, Elizabeth Falcone, Rev. James Forbes, Stephen Gillers, Jennifer Haus, Rev. James Hightower, Walter Hooke, Phoebe Hoss, Michele Host, Gwen Jordan, Sandra Kitt, Lisa Lynch, Peggy Nagae, Pamela Newkirk, Rev. Jefferson P. Rogers, Anjana Samant, Richard Simon, Donald Stocks, and Patricia Williams. John

Sexton, recently chosen as the new president of New York University, who as the dean of its law school generously provided me a place to teach and write, has been an unwavering friend and supporter.

My publisher Bloomsbury USA has been extraordinary and continues to amaze me with the commitment, creativity, and graciousness of everyone on their team. Alan Wherry, Karen Rinaldi, Colin Dickerman, and Sandee Yuen really are living embodiments of ethical ambition, and from its inception have brought a vital energy and commitment to the project. I am grateful, too, for the efforts of all on the staff, including Andrea Lynch and Alona Fryman.

Since this book is a meditation, writing it has given me the opportunity to reflect on the richness of my life and how it has been made so by my family – my parents, my late wife Jewel, our sons, Derrick, Douglass, and Carter, and extended family too numerous to mention. Janet Dewart Bell, my wife and partner, has been a major support throughout the genesis of this book. Her editor's eye and constant love provide invaluable support and encouragement.

NOTES

1 Irving Kolodin, Liner Notes, *The Beloved Bjoerling: Vol. 3, Opera Arias, 1936–1945* (Capitol Records, 1961).
2 See Paul Tillich, *The Courage to Be*, 2nd ed. (New Haven: Yale University Press, 2000).
3 Peter J. Gomes, Introduction, ibid., p. xxiii.
4 Joel Greenberg, "Protesting Tactics in West Bank, Israeli Reservists Refuse to Serve," *New York Times* (February 2, 2002), p. A1.
5 By June, 2002, the number of Israeli Army "Refuseniks" had increased to 467. Their statement, together with their names, ranks, and units, can be found at: http://www.coalitionofwomen4peace.org
6 Howard Thurman, *Deep Is the Hunger: Meditations for Apostles of Sensitiveness* (New York: Harper & Row, 1951), pp. 7–8.
7 See Bari-Ellen Roberts, *Roberts vs. Texaco: A True Story of Race and Corporate America* (New York: Avon, 1998).
8 Ibid., p. 276.
9 Greg Winter, "Coca-Cola Still Faces Suits in Race Discrimination Case," *New York Times* (July 3, 2001), p. C3.
10 See S. Jonathan Bass, *Blessed Are the Peacemakers: Martin Luther King, Jr., Eight White Religious Leaders, and the "Letter from Birgmingham Jail"* (Baton Rouge: Louisiana State University Press, 2002).
11 *A Testament of Hope: The Essential Writings and Speeches of Martin Luther King, Jr.*, James Melvin Washington, ed. (Harper San Francisco, 1986), pp. 313–314.
12 Quoted in Howard Thurman, *Jesus and the Disinherited* (Boston: Beacon Press, 1976), p. 70.
13 Nikos Kazantzakis, *The Last Temptation of Christ* (New York: Bantam, 1961), p. 419.

14 John Shelby Spong, *Born of a Woman: A Bishop Rethinks the Virgin Birth and the Treatment of Women by a Male-Dominated Church* (New York: HarperCollins, 1992), p. 6.

15 Peter Gomes, *The Good Book: Reading the Bible with Mind and Heart* (New York: Morrow, 1996), p. xii.

16 Peter Laarman, "But Is It True?" *Judson News Notes* 1 (January–February 2001).

17 Thurman, *Jesus and the Disinherited*, pp. 33, 45.

18 See Elaine Pagels, *The Gnostic Gospels* (New York: Random House, 1979).

19 Ibid., pp. xix–xx.

20 Ibid., p. 135.

21 Lois Smith Brady, "Life's Big Ricochet: From Wedding to Marriage," *New York Times* (May 27, 2002), sec. 9, pp. 1, 7.

22 John Hope Franklin and Aurelia Whittington Franklin, *For Better, for Worse* (privately published, 1999).

23 Patrick J. Schiltz, "On Being a Happy, Healthy, and Ethical Member of an Unhappy, Unhealthy, and Unethical Profession," 52 *Vand. L. Rev.* 871, 937–38 (1999).

24 Ibid., p. 910.

25 Phillip McGuire, *He Too Spoke for Democracy: Judge Hastie, World War II, and the Black Soldier* (Greenwood Publishing Group, 1988), pp. 84–85 (quoting editorial, *New York Amsterdam Star-News*, February 6, 1943). See also Gilbert Ware, *William Hastie: Grace Under Pressure* (New York: Oxford University Press, 1984).

26 Maria L. La Ganga, John M. Glionna, "Storm Greets Lone Dissenter in Vote to Broaden Bush's Powers Aftermath," *Los Angeles Times* (September 22, 2001), p. A2.

27 Michelle Locke, "Dissenter Wins Warm Applause: Berkeley Welcomes Congresswoman Who Cast a 'No' Vote on War After Sept. 11," *San Jose Mercury News* (March 19, 2002), p. B4.

28 See Aaron Henry with Constance Henry, *Aaron Henry: The Fire Burning* (Jackson, Miss.: University Press of Mississippi, 2000).

29 See Myrlie Evers et al., *For Us, the Living* (Jackson, Miss.: University Press of Mississippi, 1996).

30 http://www.bartleby.com/66/47/15947.html

31 Jo Cottrell, *Man of Destiny: The Story of Muhammad Ali* (London: Frederick Muller Press, 1967), p. 335; cited in Arthur Ashe, *A Hard Road to Glory: A History of the African-American Athlete Since 1946* (New York: Warner, 1988), p. 98.

32 David Garrow, *Bearing the Cross: Martin Luther King, Jr., and the Southern Christian Leadership Conference* (New York: Morrow, 1986), p. 564.

33 Richard Severo, "Larry Adler, Political Exile Who Brought the Harmonica to the Concert Stage, Dies at 87," *New York Times* (August 8, 2001), p. A15.

34 See, e.g., David Robinson, *Chaplin: His Life and Art* (New York: McGraw-Hill, revised ed., 1987).

35 See Paul Robeson, *Here I Stand* (Boston: Beacon Press, 1988). See also Martin Duberman, *Paul Robeson* (New York: Knopf, 1988); Paul Robeson, Jr., *The Undiscovered Paul Robeson: An Artist's Journey, 1898–1939* (New York: John Wiley & Sons, 2001).

36 Mary Duziak, *Cold War Civil Rights: Race and the Image of American Democracy* (Princeton, N.J.: Princeton University Press, 2000), pp. 100–103, 107–114; David Levering Lewis, *W.E.B. Du Bois: The Fight for Equality and the American Century, 1919–1963* (New York: Henry Holt, 2000), pp. 546–553. See also David Levering Lewis, *W.E.B. Du Bois: Biography of a Race, 1868–1919* (New York: Henry Holt, 1993).

38 Lee, Eric Ilhyung, "Nomination of Derrick A. Bell, Jr. to Be an Associate Justice of the Supreme Court of the United States: The Chronicles of a Civil Rights Activist," 22 *Ohio Northern University Law Review* (1995), pp. 363–448.

39 Chuck Culpepper, "She Is Hated by Lovers of Touchdowns," *The Oregonian* (February 28, 2001), p. F01.

40 E-mail from Linda Bensel-Meyers, February 12, 2001.

41 Faye Wattleton, *Life on the Line* (New York: Ballantine, 1996), p. 209.

42 Quoted in Pagels, *The Gnostic Gospels*, p. 126.

43 Mitch Albom, *Tuesdays with Morrie: An Old Man, a Young Man, and Life's Greatest Lesson* (New York: Doubleday, 1997), pp. 80–82.

44 Patricia Williams, *The Alchemy of Race and Rights* (Cambridge: Harvard University Press, 1991), p. 163.

45 James Russell Lowell, "The Present Crisis," www.bartleby.com/102/128.html

46 *The Autobiography of W.E.B. Du Bois* (International Publishers, 1968), p. 398.

A NOTE ON THE AUTHOR

Derrick Bell is one of the most highly respected constitutional law professors in America. His civil rights career began when Thurgood Marshall recruited him fresh out of law school. He was the first African American to be tenured at Harvard Law School, as well as the only academic to relinquish a coveted tenured position to protest Harvard Law School's failure to appoint women of color. He served as the dean of the University of Oregon Law School and again resigned when the faculty refused to hire a qualified Asian American woman. He has received several honorary degrees and currently teaches constitutional law at New York University School of Law, where the annual Derrick Bell Lecture Series was established in his honor. He has also been honored as the Annual Tobriner Memorial Lecturer and the University of California, Davis, Edward L. Barrett Jr Lecturer on Constitutional Law, and has been voted Teacher of the Year by the prestigious Society of American Law Teachers.

His legal articles have appeared in such prestigious journals as *Harvard Law Review, Yale Law Journal, NYU Review of Law and Social Change, Hastings Law Journal, UCLA Law*

Review, University of Michigan Law Review, and *Howard University Law Journal.* He has been published and/or featured in the *New York Times, Essence, USA Today, Time* magazine, *People, The Chronicle of Higher Education, Los Angeles Times, The Nation, The Village Voice, Houston Chronicle,* and *Baltimore Sun,* to name a few. He has also appeared on such national television programs as *The Charlie Rose Show, ABC World News Tonight, NBC Nightly News, CBS Evening News,* and on the cable networks C-SPAN and CNN.

He is the author of seven books, including *New York Times* best-seller *Faces from the Bottom of the Well; Afrolantica Legacies; Gospel Choirs: Psalms of Survival in an Alien Land Called Home; Confronting Authority: Reflections of an Ardent Protester; And We Are Not Saved: The Elusive Quest for Racial Justice; Race, Racism and American Law;* and *Constitutional Conflicts.*

A NOTE ON THE TYPE

The text of this book is set in Bembo. This type was first used in 1495 by the Venetian printer Aldus Manutius for Cardinal Bembo's *De Aetna*, and was cut for Manutius by Francesco Griffo. It was one of the types used by Claude Garamond (1480–1561) as a model for his Romain de L'Université, and so it was the forerunner of what became standard European type for the following two centuries. Its modern form follows the original types and was designed for Monotype in 1929.